Explaining in the Secondary School

E. C. Wragg and G. Brown

London and New York

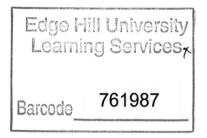
First published as *Explaining* in 1993
by Routledge
This new revised edition first published 2001
by RoutledgeFalmer
11 New Fetter Lane, London EC4P 4EE

Simultaneously published in the USA and Canada
by RoutledgeFalmer
29 West 35th Street, New York, NY 10001

RoutledgeFalmer is an imprint of the Taylor & Francis Group

© 2001 E. C. Wragg and G. Brown

Typeset in Palatino by Bookcraft Ltd, Stroud, Gloucestershire
Printed and bound in Great Britain by Bell & Bain Ltd, Glasgow

British Library Cataloguing in Publication Data
A catalogue record for this book is available from the British Library

Library of Congress Cataloging in Publication Data
Wragg, E. C. (Edward Conrad)
   Explaining in the secondary school / E. C. Wragg and G. Brown.
      p. cm. – (Successful teaching series)
   'First published as Explaining in 1993'–T.p. verso
   Includes bibliographical references (p.).
      1. High school teaching. 2. Explanation. I. Brown, George,
   1935– II. Wragg, E. C. (Edward Conrad). Explaining. III. Title.
   IV. Successful teaching series (London, England)

   LB1607. W73 2001
   373.1102–dc21   00–051795

ISBN 0–415–24956–2

Contents

Preface

Improving the quality of learning in secondary schools, and preparing children for what will probably be a long and complex life in the twenty-first century, requires the highest quality of teaching and professional training. The *Successful Teaching Series* focuses on the essence of classroom competence, on those professional skills that make a real difference to children, such as the ability to explain clearly, to ask intelligent and thought-provoking questions, to manage classes effectively and to use the assessment of progress to enhance pupils' learning.

'Success' may be defined in many ways. For some it is seen purely in test scores, for others it is a broader issue, involving the whole child. In this series we report what teachers have done that has been judged to be successful or unsuccessful. To do this several criteria have been used: headteachers' assessments, pupil progress measures, esteem from fellow teachers or from children. Skilful teachers ensure that their classes learn something worthwhile; unskilful teachers may turn off that delicate trip-switch in children's psyche which keeps their minds open to lifelong learning.

Experienced teachers engage in hundreds of exchanges every single day of their career, thousands in a year, millions over a professional lifetime. Teaching consists of dozens of favoured strategies that become embedded in deep structures, for there is no time to re-think every single move in a busy classroom. Many decisions are made by teachers in less than a second, so once these *deep structures* have been laid down they are not always amenable to change, even if a school has a well-developed professional development programme. Reflecting on practice alone or with colleagues does enable teachers to think about what they do away from the immediate pressures of rapid interaction and speedy change.

Rejecting the notion that there is only one way to teach, this series of books explores some of the many strategies available to teachers, as well as the patterns of classroom organisation which best assist pupil learning. It demonstrates that teachers, even when working to predetermined work schemes and curricula, must forge their own ways of teaching in the light of the context in which they operate and the evidence available to them from different sources. The series is rooted in classroom observation research over several decades and is designed to assist teachers at all stages of their professional development.

The series also contains an element that is unusual in most of the books that are aimed at helping teachers. Some of the activities assume that teaching should not just be something that teachers do *to* their pupils, but rather *with* them, so the exercises involve teachers and their classes working together to improve teaching and learning; pupils acting as partners, not merely as passive recipients of professional wizardry. Thus the books on class management consider such matters as self-discipline; those on questioning and explaining look at pupils interacting with each other; those on assessment address how children can learn from being assessed and also how they can appraise their own work. When children become adults they will have to be able to act autonomously, so it is crucial that they learn early to take more and more responsibility for their own progress.

The books are useful for:

- practising teachers;
- student teachers;
- college and university tutors, local and national inspectors and advisers;
- school-based in-service co-ordinators, advisory teachers;
- school mentors, appraisers and headteachers.

Like the others in the series, this book can be used as part of initial or in-service programmes in school. Individuals can use it as a source of ideas, and it is helpful in teacher appraisal, in developing professional awareness both for those being appraised and for their appraisers. The suggested activities have been tried out extensively by experienced teachers and those in pre-service training and have been revised in the light of their comments.

The series will provoke discussion, help teachers reflect on their current and future practice and encourage them to look behind, and ask questions about, everyday classroom events.

Acknowledgements

Our thanks to the many members of our research teams, especially Gill Haynes, Caroline Wragg, Rosemary Chamberlin, Felicity Wikeley, Kay Wood, Sarah Crowhurst, Clive Carré, Trevor Kerry, Pauline Dooley, Allyson Trotter, Barbara Janssen, Sheila Armstrong and Rowena Edmondson, who between them have observed over two thousand lessons and interviewed teachers, pupils, parents and classroom assistants in hundreds of primary and secondary schools.

We should also like to express our gratitude to the many teachers who teach successfully on a daily basis. A number of the teachers shown at work in the books in the *Successful Teaching Series* are recipients of Platos, which are given to the national winners at the annual Teaching Awards ceremony.

The photographs in this book were taken by Fred Jarvis and Ted Wragg. The cartoons are by Jonathan Hall.

Aims and content

The ability to explain clearly is a vital human talent, recognised and appreciated as such by children as young as two or three. Most of us at some time or another need an explanation, whether we are young or old. Every day millions of people explain something to millions of other people. A policeman will tell a bewildered visitor how to find a tourist attraction; a doctor may tell a patient what diabetes is and how to cope with it; a parent will explain to a small child why it is dangerous to play too near the fire. In addition to these explanations outside the school system, there will be thousands of teachers working in classrooms who will explain a new concept, or a classroom rule, who will clarify confusion, whet someone's appetite for more, maybe unlock a mystery. This book attempts to help new teachers learn how to master the art of clear explanation and to help experienced teachers to improve their skills at explaining.

At the beginning of a lesson, a teacher will often spend five or ten minutes setting up what might be an hour's, a day's, a week's or even a term's work, so time invested in establishing or improving the ability to explain is time well spent. Badly handled, this setting-up phase may be followed by mayhem, as children, uncertain what they are supposed to do, or why they should do it, resort to asking one another, improvising or simply hoping the teacher will explain the task once more. Well conducted, however, a good explanation or introduction can motivate a class very effectively.

We once carried out a case study of a teacher who was shown in a research project to have secured the highest gains in learning of any teacher in the sample. Her explanations were a pleasure to witness. On one occasion she was telling a group of children about a maths worksheet on which they were about to embark.

Many teachers would have simply handed the worksheets round and told pupils to get on with it, but she drew their attention to one or two of the questions, warned them that one particular question was tricky, reminded them of the principles on which the exercise was based, checked they all understood and concluded with, 'I can't wait to see what you make of number five'. The speed and enthusiasm with which the group commenced was more reminiscent of the quest for the Holy Grail than completion of a maths worksheet.

The book is organised into the following six units:

In **Unit 1** we discuss what an explanation actually is, what it consists of, its manifold purposes and the viewpoint of pupils.

Unit 2 investigates the various strategies employed by people when explaining, including the use of questions, the type of structure to be found in explanations and the use of ancillary aids.

Unit 3 explores levels of explanation, the analysis of explaining using observation schedules and other approaches, and also the need to match explanations to individuals and groups.

Unit 4 touches on important aspects of any explanation – that is, its actual content, the subject matter it covers, and the coping strategies that are developed, given that teachers cannot have in their grasp all the knowledge in the world.

Unit 5 describes strategies for explaining that appear to be effective if skilfully employed – the use of an appropriate language register; the place of analogies; the qualities of clarity and fluency; the ability to listen and use pupils' ideas.

Unit 6 concentrates on the evaluation of explanations, the kind of feedback that is available, the assessment of learning, and ways to improve one's own teaching in the light of experience.

HOW TO USE THIS BOOK

The six units constitute substantial course material for the topic 'explaining'. The activities and text are suitable for in-service and professional studies courses as well as for individual use.

The text may be read as a book in its own right; all the *activities* can be undertaken either by individual teachers or by members of a group working together on the topic.

The discussion activities can be used in group meetings, for example, or as part of staff discussion during a school's INSET day. The individual reader can use these as a prompt for reflection and planning.

The written activities are intended to be worked on individually but also lend themselves to group discussion when completed.

The practical activities are designed to be done in the teacher's own classroom or by student teachers on teaching practice or when they are teaching children brought into the training institution for professional work.

The book can either be used alone or in conjunction with other books in the *Successful Teaching Series*. Those responsible for courses, therefore, may well wish to put together exercises and activities from several of the books in this series to make up their own course as part of a general professional skills development programme, either in initial training or of whole school professional development. Usually the discussion and written activities described will occupy between an hour and ninety minutes and classroom activities completed in about an hour, though this may vary, depending on the context.

Many of the issues covered in this book are generic and apply to both primary and secondary teaching. Most of the illustrations and examples cited are from the appropriate phase of schooling, but in certain cases they are taken from another year group, either for the sake of clarity, or because the original research work referred to was done with that particular age cohort of pupils.

Unit 1   What is explaining?

A brilliant explanation of a concept or process can change someone's life. A teacher we once interviewed in a research project described vividly how his own former teacher, explaining the symbiotic relationship between ants and aphids, had awakened an interest in and curiosity about science that had led to him becoming a science graduate and wanting to teach the subject himself. The effects of good explaining can be significant and far-reaching.

Explaining is not a single type of activity. The words 'explain' and 'explanation' can be used in different ways. Consider these four statements:

'Why are you two messing about when I've already told you once not to? I want an explanation.'

'Miss, can you explain how to do this sum?'

'You've just been told by the garage that you'll have to buy a new battery? That explains why your car wouldn't start.'

'Can you give me an explanation of why water freezes in winter?'

In the first statement, the quest for an 'explanation' is probably a prelude to a reprimand. The children are not really being asked for an account of personality factors, genetic endowment or environmental influences on their personal and social development. Just imagine the teacher's reaction if the child's 'explanation' began, 'According to experts on ethnology, rough-and-tumble play is a well-documented feature in the behaviour of young primates.' In this context, the request for an 'explanation' is expected to produce a feeble justification or an apology. In the second example, the response may be a brief clarification and reminder of a specific technique already learned, such as how to solve a maths problem using fractions, or it may involve a fundamental explanation of what a particular mathematical transaction involves, to a pupil who has no understanding whatsoever of it. The third example, on the other hand, is the identification of a simple relationship between cause and effect: the car would not start owing to a dying battery. In the fourth case, the 'explanation' offered by a pupil could vary enormously in complexity. A satisfactory answer from a 6-year-old might be that water freezes 'because it's very cold in winter'. A 12-year-old might be expected to say, 'because the temperature has dropped below freezing point, which is 0 degrees centigrade'. A Nobel prizewinner might write a treatise on the structure of matter at differing temperatures, which could be incomprehensible to the lay audience.

We shall take as our operational definition, therefore, the statement: 'Explaining is giving understanding to another.'

This definition takes for granted that there are numerous contexts in which this may occur, many forms that explanations may take, and varying degrees of, and criteria for, success. Cruickshank and Metcalf (1994) put forward three types of explanations, dealing with concepts, procedures, or rules. We take a broader view, believing that an explanation can help someone understand, among other matters:

concepts   including those which are new or familiar to the learner, like 'density' or 'prejudice';

cause and effect   that rain is produced by the cooling of air, that a flat battery causes car-starting problems;

procedures   classroom rules, homework requirements, how to convert a fraction to a decimal, how to ensure safety during gymnastics;

purposes and objectives   why children are studying the topic, what they can expect to have learned at the conclusion of a particular task;

relationships   between people, things or events: why footballers and pop-stars are both called (sometimes mistakenly) 'entertainers'; why flies and bees are insects, but spiders are not; what are the common features of festivals, like Christmas, Diwali, Passover;

processes   how machines work, how animals or people behave.

There are numerous other kinds of explanation, and also there are variations of the categories given above. For example, explaining *consequences* can be similar, but is not necessarily identical to *cause and effect* explanation. The *consequence* of putting your hand into scalding water will be intense pain and a visit to the hospital. A *cause and effect* explanation might concentrate on how intense heat destroys tissue and what causes pain, but an explanation of *consequences* might look at such matters as the foolishness of an action, its effect on others as well as the victim, and the cost in time and money of treating self-imposed injury. Furthermore, some explanations can cover more than one category. Explaining to a class what the Roman wall is, could involve *concepts* ('aggression', 'defence'), *cause and effect* (what led to the wall being built), *processes* and *procedures* (how the wall was built, on whose authority) and *purposes* (to keep out the enemy).

Activity 1

A group of student or experienced teachers are working together to look at how explanations can be improved. Let a member of the group choose a hobby or interest he or she has. Just *one* key aspect of this interest should then be explained to the rest, taking no more than four or five minutes. There are countless possibilities, such as: what I like about chess; my favourite twentieth-century building; a simple recipe; getting rid of litter; how to lose weight; an effective advert; why lifeboats don't sink; the best (or worst) thing about being a parent, or having an older brother/sister; home insulation or the play/piece of music/poem/ painting that moved me most.

Analyse the nature of the explanation, using, if possible, an audio- or video-tape of it. What were the key concepts? What types of explanation were involved? How effective an explanation was it, and why?

Audience

Those who receive the explanation must be an important consideration, so consider what differences and similarities there might have been if the explanation had been directed to:

- an 11-year-old with slight learning difficulties;
- a bright 14-year-old;
- an intelligent Martian.

Let the person have a second attempt at explaining a different topic, or the same one, in the light of feedback.

MAIN FEATURES OF EXPLANATIONS

Keys

Activity 1 should demonstrate a number of fundamental features of effective explaining. First of all there are several *keys* which help to unlock understanding. A *key* may be a central principle or a generalisation. It may contain an example, or an analogy. For instance, if someone were describing a recipe for making an omelette, then the notion of *heat* would be central. If too little heat is applied eggs will not set, if too much, then the eggs will burn and the omelette will resemble a cork tablemat.

It is not too difficult to see other *keys* to understanding how to cook an omelette. The question of *taste* will occur, and thus the addition of flavourings like salt and pepper, or fillings like cheese or mushroom. *Texture* is also important, hence the need to beat the eggs so that yolk and white mix evenly and to introduce air so the omelette will be light. The great chef Escoffier used to put little pieces of butter into the egg mixture which melted during cooking and affected both taste and texture, so this might be a concrete example used to illustrate one or more of the central notions or keys in the explanation. Where omelettes are concerned, the difference between a good and a bad explanation could be the difference between an Escoffier masterpiece and a poultice. Introduce a key concept like *health* and the need to avoid too much salt and too many dairy products, and to cook eggs to a certain temperature to prevent salmonella, and you may not have your omelette at all!

Voice and gesture can amplify explanations

Voice and gesture can amplify explanations

There is more to an explanation, however, than a bunch of keys. The *voice* of the explainer is important. The same text read by someone with a pleasant, well-modulated voice and another person with a flat, tedious delivery, will sound quite different. The correct use of voice involves light and shade, knowing when to slow down or accelerate, which words or phrases to emphasise, when to pause and how to 'read' the audience so that the appropriate tone of voice is used: hushed for something serious, lighter for the frivolous or humorous. Sometimes voice is amplified by gesture such as pointing to something or spreading arms to indicate size or breadth. Gestures may be difficult for those who feel inhibited, but, well used, can offer an amplification of the voice. Imagine you are doing a radio broadcast about teaching science in the primary school. Try saying the following sentence in different tones of voice:

> 'Science can be very exciting for children, because they'll learn about some of the most spectacular phenomena in the universe; but, if they're badly taught, science will seem a tedious chore.'

If you speak the words in a flat monotone, it will sound as dreary as the condemnation of bad teaching suggests. For effective communication you may choose to emphasise words like 'exciting', 'spectacular' or 'badly'. You may pause after 'but' and slow down on the words 'tedious chore'. Your voice may rise in pitch during the 'exciting' first half of the statement, and fall at the dreary foreboding of the second part.

Structure and purpose

There are several aspects of *structure* that are important. If an explanation has several keys in it – maybe three or four principal features that need to be brought out – then thought must be given to such matters as the *sequence* of ideas: how you should begin, which notion should be unwrapped or explored first, which second, which left till last and how you might conclude the explanation. These matters cannot always be fully determined in advance, because once pupils become engaged by an explanation, their questions, insights, confusion or suggestions will begin to take over and affect the process.

Questions about *structure* are closely related to those about *teaching strategies*. What use should be made of questions? (See the companion book in this series on *Questioning in the Secondary School* by the same authors.) What is the place of a demonstration? Of practical work by the children? Of individual, group or whole-class teaching? How much and what sort of practice may be needed if the children are learning a concept, such as what a fraction is, or a skill, like how to shape a piece of wood with a file? What sort of aids to teaching might help: a picture; a video; a model or a piece of equipment?

In turn, thoughts about *teaching strategies* are partly contingent on the *purpose* of the explanation. Is it to teach a fact; a skill; a concept; a form of attitude or behaviour? In health education, for example, if children are learning about dental care, then one principal objective would be to ensure that they clean their teeth and avoid tooth decay.

The teacher may have to explain *facts* (what causes tooth decay, what prevents it, such as regular brushing, avoiding certain foods, using fluoride toothpaste and anti-plaque mouthwash); *skills* such as how to clean your teeth properly (trendy dentists nowadays recommend circular movements of the brush to follow the shape of the gum, rather than just side to side, or up and down); *attitudes*, like why it is worth cleaning your teeth properly (it is preferable to pain); and *behaviour* (ensuring that children really do clean their teeth, rather than just appear sanctimonious about it). The payoff for successful explaining of the first three – facts, skills and attitudes – would be the last, that is, ensuring behaviour which avoided needless decay and discomfort, so that the purpose of explanations in health education is often clear, even if results are difficult to achieve.

The 'tease'

Within a certain overall purpose there may be a set of shorter-term objectives. For example, in order to give an explanation of how to avoid dental decay, the teacher may decide to make the opening gambit one which will arouse interest or intrigue the class, saying, 'In a minute I'm going to tell you why my uncle can't eat raspberries and walnuts any more, even though he loves them, but first I want to know if anyone's ever had toothache.' This device is known as a *'tease'* in broadcasting, and many radio and television programmes begin with a tease: 'And in a packed programme today we'll be meeting the man who can play the oboe underwater, and we'll be telling you how you can save thousands of pounds without effort, but first the news headlines.' It is one of many ways of both gaining attention and shaping the presentation of information.

Activity 2

1   Imagine you are starting a project on 'Nutrition and Health' with a class of children aged about thirteen, which might run for four or five weeks. Decide how you might explain what 'Nutrition' actually involves, asking yourself:

(a)   What are the key concepts children will need to understand (e.g. care of the teeth? need for food for activity and growth?).

(b)   How could I find out what children already know?

(c)   How would I introduce the topic?

(d)   What sort of strategies, activities, materials would I need?

2   Compare your ideas with those of others in your group. What is in common and what is different? Have you identified similar key concepts/strategies?

3   Try out your idea with a group of children if you have the opportunity; you can modify it, as appropriate, if you can only have them for a short period of time. Look at the following:

(a)   Did the children already know more or less about 'Nutrition' than you thought they would?

(b)   How effectively did they learn the key concepts?

(c)   Would they, for example, be able to write or talk about human energy or about what benefits and what harms our bodies?

(d)   If you have been able to make an audio-tape or video-tape of your session, are there any interesting events worthy of further thought – a good question you or a child asked, someone being puzzled, a good illustrative example you used?

(e)   How would you explain the topic next time in the light of your experience?

THE PUPIL'S PERSPECTIVE

The most scintillating explanation can be wasted if the audience does not understand, or knows the facts already and so is deeply bored. There are usually at least two parties in an explanation, the explainer and what you might call the 'explainee', the person to whom something is being explained. Adult life is full of such pairs, and sometimes, as in classroom teaching, explanations can be reciprocal: person A explains to person B, and then, in turn, person B explains to person A.

A doctor may begin a consultation by asking the patient to explain the pain or the symptoms causing concern. At this point the patient is the explainer. Once the doctor has made a diagnosis, roles are reversed and the doctor now explains the nature of the ailment to the patient. A similar process occurs when we call in someone to mend our car or television set and, in the classroom, when children explain to their teacher what it is they do not understand.

We once ran a training session with a group of teacher trainees. The students each took about ten children and had to introduce a topic like 'Sea Travel' or

'Volcanoes' in any way they chose. They were then video-taped and, following analysis of the video, were able to have a second chance with a different but similar-sized group of children from the same class.

In her first attempt, Helen, a conscientious student, launched her carefully prepared model of a volcano with a torrent of information: 'Today I want to tell you a little bit about volcanoes. Here is a model of one and you can see that this is the crater and, as you probably know, this is the lava, and this part here is called the magma chamber. Perhaps you've heard of volcanoes before. There's one in Italy called Vesuvius … '

Seeing the lack of opportunity for the children to respond to her 'as you probably know' and 'perhaps you've heard of' statements, in her second attempt she showed the children her model and asked if anyone knew anything about volcanoes. To her surprise a collection of information began to emerge from this new group of children, things seen on television, or learned from books, friends or relatives, that went way beyond what she had told the first group of children. Some mention was made of Vesuvius, Etna, Krakatoa and the volcanic dust that travelled round the world, Surtsey, craters on the moon, Icelandic geysers and Tristan da Cunha, and terms like 'lava' and 'eruption' emerged naturally. This approach gave her a much clearer idea of the level at which to pitch the explanation of volcanoes and volcanic activity, as well as an indication of which children had a sophisticated understanding of the topic and which needed a basic grounding.

One reason for trying to elicit from the pupils what they already know is to help with the choice of a suitable *language register*. Doctors have to make decisions everyday about what words and phrases to use with patients who have different backgrounds. Some may cope easily with medical terms, others may need analogies ('It's like a car running out of petrol') or more familiar everyday language ('waterworks', instead of 'urinary tract'). With adult learners or older secondary school pupils, a teacher might readily use a phrase like 'inversely proportional' in a maths or physics lesson, assuming the class would understand. For pupils not yet able to grasp abstract concepts, however, the teacher might say, 'The more you have of this, the less you have of that', or with anyone who needed a concrete analogy, 'It's like a seesaw: the higher you are on this side, the lower someone is on that one.'

Another strong reason for establishing what pupils already understand about a new topic or concept prior to a course of explanation is to clarify any misconceptions that might occur. Suppose, for example, you were teaching about floating and sinking. If you simply gave pupils experiments to do, or delivered a short lecturette on the topic, you might not realise that some had acquired incorrect assumptions which needed to be unlearned. Even a simple opening question like, 'Which things float in water and which things sink?' might reveal that some children wrongly believe that heavy objects invariably sink and light objects always float. Yet a 1,000-ton ship floats and a tiny pebble sinks.

Knowing about misconceptions provides valuable information prior to an explanation. As the cartoon on the following page shows, failure to appreciate the impact of an explanation because the explainer is unaware how complex it appears to the recipient, or uses the wrong language, or does not appreciate what the learner understands or misunderstands, can be a disaster. The explainer can be very pleased with, from his vantage point, an explanation that has been clearly delivered, yet the poor beggar who is supposed to be enlightened can be left feeling utterly confused. Pupils acquire thousands of misconceptions which skilful explainers can detect and correct. Many pupils believe, for example, that volcanic lava comes from the centre of the earth (it doesn't, it comes from the mantle).

Most important of all, from the pupils' point of view, explaining has often been shown to be the skill most appreciated by pupils. A study of several thousand pupils in Birmingham in the 1930s showed that, of a list of seven teaching skills, the ability to explain clearly was placed first. Fifty years later we conducted another survey of 200 pupils, this time using a list of thirty-two teaching skills, and again the ability to explain was in first place (Wragg, 1989).

SUMMARY

Explaining is the giving of understanding to another. It can involve children learning about:

- concepts;
- cause and effect;
- procedures;
- purposes and objectives;
- relationships;
- processes;
- consequences;
- a host of other notions.

Unlocking understanding may be done in numerous ways. These include:

- the identification of keys (central concepts, principles);
- effective use of voice and gesture;
- clearly structured explanations;
- proper sequencing of ideas and linking of keys;
- deployment of a range of strategies to teach knowledge, skills attitudes and behaviour;
- using appropriate teaching aids.

The pupil's perspective is especially important. To avoid confusion try to:

- find out what individual children already know and understand about the topic or concept;
- use an appropriate language register with sensible choice of words and phrases appropriate to the context;
- find out about misconceptions which need to be unlearned.

Other units in this book will cover some of these matters in greater detail. To conclude this section, try the following activity either alone or with others. It brings together some of the points covered in this unit.

Activity 3

1   Look out for examples of the following in your own teaching or in that of another teacher or student you are observing. Make brief notes after your lesson (or during the lesson if you are observing someone else) in the spaces below.

(a)   An explanation of a concept:

(b)   An explanation of a procedure:

(c)   A key point in an explanation:

(d)   An example of a child's misconception or erroneous view of something:

(e)   A particular word or phrase which needed to be clarified for a pupil:

2   Consider how effectively each of these was handled, what the teacher did and what the pupil(s) did.
3   If you are in a group, discuss your notes with others who have done the same sort of analysis.

Unit 2 Strategies of explanation

Explanations are invoked by many different causes. They may be given in answer to questions, sometimes actual questions which children have asked, like:

'Why do you sometimes say *blanc* and other times *blanche* in French?'

'How can you take 45 away from 29? It's too small, it can't be done. You'd have to switch them round, wouldn't you?'

'Where are the Himalayas on this map?'

Teachers give some explanations in answer to hypothetical questions, as, for example, when they explain what the children will do on a field trip they have arranged (destination, purpose, accommodation, clothing needed), even though no one may yet have enquired about the detail. Indeed the common interrogatives Who? What? How? Why? Where? When? – offer clues to the nature of different types of explanation.

'Who?' questions often produce explanations of relationships. An account of the Normans in Britain might explain who they were and the fact that their relationship with Britons was as conquerors.

'How?' questions, on the other hand, may lead to an evaluation of a process. Exploration of how people in a neighbourhood earn their living could involve learning about farming, factory work or transportation.

'Why?' questions lead to an understanding of purposes and objectives. If a teacher were asked to explain why babies cry, this could involve such reasons as 'to signal pain', 'to obtain food', 'to express frustration' and so on.

Most of these explanations in answer to interrogatives are not of a single kind. A 'Why?' question might equally provoke an explanation of a process, not just a purpose. Many scientific 'Why?' questions, like 'Why does a magnet pick up iron?' or 'Why do things fall down and not up?' elicit an explanation that covers both a process and a concept, such as 'gravity'. Wrapped inside a 'Why?' question is often a 'How?' question.

Activity 4

The teacher is trying to explain how animals avoid drying out, using a sponge and a plastic bag containing water. This particular explanation led to some confusion in pupils' minds, so why do you think this was?

T: Listen a minute. I'm going to show you – I'm going to show in this bag … It's got a wet sponge in it and that is like the inside of a mealworm. Can you see the inside of the bag?

P: It's leaking.

T: I hope not.

P: Water.

P: Drops.

T: Water. You feel the outside of that bag. What is it?

P: Nothing.

T: Nothing?

P: Dry.

T: Dry. So how do you think the mealworm stops itself from losing water? How do you think – if it's wet inside and dry on the outside – how do you think the mealworm stops itself from losing water?

P: Because the condensation inside cools him down.

T: No, we're talking about how he stops himself from losing water.

P: Gets too hot.

P: Overdoes it.

T: Yes, but what do you think the polythene bag's like? What do you think it's like? What do you wear in wet weather?

P: A mackintosh.

T: A mackintosh.

P: Polythene.

T: Polythene, that's right. So how do you think the polythene bag stops?

P: It stops the water getting in.

T: And out! The polythene bag acts like a waterproof coat, doesn't it?

P: But the sponge soaks it up.

T: The sponge soaks it up and so the water's held in the tissues in the mealworm, isn't it?

Look at the *strategies* employed by both the teacher and the pupils which might develop or hinder understanding. What is clear and what is vague? (For example, 'Because the condensation inside cools him down' is a thoughtful answer that is turned down without explanation.)

DIFFERENT APPROACHES

During our research projects we have often asked several teachers to explain the same topic or concept to their class. It was most interesting to see the range of explanations and the variety of strategies employed. One of the topics was 'Insects' and here are just some of the strategies employed by different teachers observed during the research project.

A factual exposition   A straightforward explanation by the teacher describing body shape, number of legs, wings, etc.

A closed question   To which there is a single, verifiable textbook answer, e.g. 'How many legs do insects have?' or 'Is a spider an insect?'

An open question   To which there are several answers, e.g. 'Who can tell me something about insects?'

A focused question   For example, 'What sort of things does an insect have on its head?' These questions may be partly open, in that there are several possible answers, yet partly closed, in the sense that the answers are verifiable as correct or incorrect, but focused specifically on one particular aspect of the explanation.

Probing questions   Sometimes teachers use a sequence of probing questions, persisting with the same line of questioning, but seeking greater depth and clarity, as, for example, in the following:

> T: What are these for?
> P: They're feelers.
> T: Yes, but what are they for?
> P: Feeling things.
> T: Yes, but what exactly do they do? What does the insect use them for?

Another example:

> T: Would you like to tell me what an insect is, Daniel?
> P: An animal with six legs.
> T: Six legs, so if I took a centipede and pulled off ninety-four legs, would that make it an insect?

Teaching specialist terms
> T: Do you know what that part of the body is called?
> P: The middle bit.
> T: No, it's got a posh word – the thorax.
> P: He's got antlers though.
> T: [smiles] *What* did you say, Simon? [laughter] He's nearly right though. What are they really called?

Teacher makes a joke about Simon confusing 'antlers' and 'antennae'.

Praise   Frequent use was observed of teachers praising correct answers or comments, either with a simple 'good' or more effusively.

Chiding   There were a few observations of reprimands for incorrect answers, usually when the pupil had not taken the issue seriously. Incorrect answers were more frequently corrected by the teacher or else another pupil was called on to correct the error.

Practical work   Pupils handled real insects, or looked at models or specimens in perspex cases. Some made insect shapes out of coloured pipe cleaners.

Pictures   Teachers gave out photographs or drawings of insects.

Analogy/example   Often teachers will give or elicit an example, 'A house-fly is an insect', or use an analogy, for example, one teacher said, 'Now, insects' eyes are rather special, not like ours. The insect's eye is made up of hundreds of separate tiny eyes, very sensitive to movement. Its eye looks almost like a plastic bag of marbles; the plastic bag is the whole eye and the marbles are the mini-eyes or lenses.'

This teacher used the 'plastic bag of marbles' as a concrete analogy. Another teacher referred to the insect's eye as being 'like banks of television sets all showing the same picture'.

'Not' analogy/example   Just as a teacher might say something is 'like' something else, so too teachers use 'not' analogies and examples as a means of contrast. Among instances were:

'Is a bird an insect?'

'What's the difference between an elephant and an insect?'

'Why is a camel not an insect?'

Involving imagination   Even in a factual explanation, some teachers involved pupils' imagination. Examples were:

'What do you think it must feel like to be an insect?'

'Do you know that butterflies can taste with their feet? [Laughter] Yes, when they land on things they can taste them using their feet. Wouldn't it be funny if we could taste with our feet!'

A 'tease'   Some teachers began their explanation with a 'tease'.

> T: If I told you that in, say, a bucket of earth there were hundreds of them. They're in the air; they're even in ponds and rivers. There are millions of them in a tree. They live all over the world, except at the North and South Poles. There are over a million different types of them. There are 200,000 different types in this country alone. Some of them can fly, some can swim, some make holes in the ground and some make holes in wood. What do you think I would be talking about?

A 'tease' need not be a superficial attention-getting gimmick. The notable feature of this 'tease' is the richness of information in it.

Practical work   Making a model of an insect.

Anecdote/story   Several teachers used a personal anecdote about a bee or a butterfly, or invited children to tell these. Some told a short story:

> T: Shall I tell you a story? Many years ago, when I was a little boy, in China the Chinese people decided to kill thousands of millions of birds because they were eating all the crops. The next spring, guess what happened. All the caterpillars ate the crops, because there were no birds to kill the caterpillars!

Summary and review

At the end of the session it was common, though not inevitable, to find some kind of summary, sometimes by the pupils, sometimes by the teachers. This topic is discussed again below, but here is an example of an interactive joint teacher and pupil summary:

Summary and review

> T: So then, let's go back to my little friend here [teacher points to model of an insect]. Who's going to tell me the names of the parts?
> P: Head.
> T: Head, yes.
> P: Thorax and abdomen.
> T: Well done. What are these?
> P: Feelers.
> T: And what are they for?
> P: Tasting the air.
> T: Yes, 'tasting' the air, that's a good description.

These many different strategies and tactics show something of the infinite range of possibilities in just one simple topic. Explaining is not a single entity, not a unidimensional monochrome skill, but rather a repertoire of skills requiring much of what teachers need in daily professional life – planning, management and organisation, the ability to ask intelligent, varied and appropriate questions, clarity, involvement of pupils, practical work, the use of teaching aids and numerous other aspects of competency.

There are many times when children are busily engaged in activities from which they are learning and they are, therefore, in a sense explaining things to themselves; but frequently, when teachers and pupils are interacting together, teaching *is* explaining. It is the single predominant purpose, so it needs to be done well.

THE BROAD STRATEGIES

In later units we shall be dealing specifically with some of the particular strategies mentioned above, but at this point it is important to reflect on some of the broad categories like preparation, openings, questioning, practical work and the use of teaching aids, the structure of explanations and summary.

Preparation and planning

Preparation for the detail of a lesson is not always possible since a great deal of what happens in teaching is spontaneous and unrehearsed, unanticipated even. When teachers begin to explain a new topic or a classroom procedure to their pupils, before long the children's responses, their questions, insights, looks of puzzlement, smiles or frowns, will, if the teacher is sensitive to them, begin to affect the nature and direction of the explanation. Consider the messages, amplifications, opportunities and distractions in this exchange with an English class of 13- and 14-year-olds who are discussing the use of similes and metaphors in the Shakespeare play *Romeo and Juliet*:

P: What's the difference between a simile and a metaphor?
T: Well, a simile is when you say something is 'like' something else: if you say 'he runs like a gazelle', or 'It's as old as the hills'. A metaphor, that's when you use a word or a phrase and it's not meant to be taken literally. If you say about a football team 'they were on fire', you just mean they were playing well, you don't mean they were literally in flames.
P: But that's the same.
T: What do you mean?
P: It's the same thing. If you say somebody runs like a gazelle, you don't mean they're a real gazelle.
P: What's a gazelle?
P: It's an animal, stupid.
T: I see what you mean, but they're not quite the same. They're similar, but they're different. With a simile you usually use the words 'like' or 'as', which you don't need with a metaphor. When Juliet says, 'My bounty is as boundless as the sea, My love as deep; the more I give to thee', that's a simile.
P: But she doesn't mean literally that her love *is* the sea, so why isn't it a metaphor?
T: Because she uses 'as', like I said. We've got to move on now, we've got a lot more to get through today.

However carefully a lesson is pre-planned, pupils' own thoughts, uncertainties and concerns are close to the surface and they are eager to express them. In the above exchanges the teacher was intending to read through a key scene in *Romeo and Juliet* and mentioned the word 'simile' in passing. In order to maintain the interest of the pupils and secure their commitment to the play, he was prepared to answer a question, though after a while he began to feel some frustration and became eager to move on.

With experience, teachers learn to make quick decisions in the course of their lessons, drawing on an ever-deeper reservoir of similar and contrasting events. As we are concentrating here on the forethought that will be necessary when planning the lesson, we take these under three headings: first-, second- and third- order considerations. Planning time is not infinite, but certain strategic matters can be thought about in advance, still leaving opportunities for spontaneity, imagination and sudden inspiration, or 'busking it', as one experienced broadcaster used to say about surviving in live television and radio when plans went amiss.

First order   The *general and most important purpose* of the activity, for example: to read, understand, enjoy and enact the play *Romeo and Juliet*. This more noble-sounding objective can still embrace within it the need to pass an examination, or do well in a national test.

Second order   What the *keys* are in the explanation? What central concepts, skills or processes need to be explained? The principal focus in this particular lesson may be on the growing love between the two central characters, Romeo and Juliet, but understanding the terms 'simile' and 'metaphor' might also be a *key*, albeit of a different type.

Third order   What *strategies* can effectively achieve these aims: what is best done with the whole group, what with a small group, what with individuals; what sort of questions might be asked; any practical activity, like an enactment of the whole or part of a scene; how to secure the commitment and interest/involvement of the pupils (how they can 'get inside' the characters, rather than merely absorb the teacher's interpretations, important though these may be); whether an initial 'tease' might work, like saying, 'In this scene we'll see the first sign that there's going to be trouble ahead. I wonder if anyone will spot it.'

The fact that teachers need to give thought to the preparation of explanations does not rule out children playing a significant part in them. Indeed, skilful teachers ensure that children's ideas and suggestions play a central role from the beginning, even though these will make the pattern of development to some extent unpredictable. Nevertheless, having initial thoughts about purpose, key notions and a deft strategy or two is a wise investment of planning time for the explaining, setting-up phase of the activity.

Openings – the 'tease' or 'advance organiser'

The opening to an explanation cannot be seen as entirely separate from the rest of it. There is no point in staging some spectacular opening move, just to find that only the gimmick is remembered. Ultimately, something important must be learned and all the opening can do is to set the scene and prepare the way for what follows.

There was an old tip given to university academics before they delivered their first lecture. It ran, 'Tell them what you're going to tell them. Tell them. Tell them what you've told them.' It was a crude tip and, judging by the lectures some of us have had to endure, often ignored, but the general shape of opening/exposition/recapitulation offered some degree of structure for what was potentially a rambling, shapeless hour of presentation.

The 'Tell them what you're going to tell them' sort of opening is sometimes referred to as an *advance organiser*. It can be especially useful when teaching individual or sets of concepts, particularly if these are complex. There is debate in educational research about how effective advance organisers are (Ausubel *et al.*, 1978), for though there is some evidence to suggest children given advance organisers achieve better understanding and higher test scores, this sort of research has not always been well conducted, and is in any case notoriously difficult to carry out, given that advance organisers are but one of several devices that teachers use. It is also open to argument that telling people what they are going to be doing in a particular lesson spoils the mystery and might even reduce their motivation.

Consider, however, the use made by the German playwright Bertolt Brecht of a narrator at the beginning of each scene in his play *Life of Galileo*. This narrator, in a few lines and often with the aid of a caption, tells the audience what is going to occur. For example, at the beginning of one scene he announces that, instead of a new age of reason dawning, based on scientific discovery, the Inquisition will make Galileo refute his own research findings about the Earth rotating around the Sun.

Does it ruin the play now that we know Galileo will recant in the coming scene, for fear of being tortured by the Inquisition? Probably no more than knowing at the beginning of Shakespeare's *Julius Caesar* that Brutus and Cassius will kill Caesar, or being told by the three witches in *Macbeth* what is going to happen next.

Openings of explanations can have several purposes, therefore:

- to organise in advance what is to come;
- to intrigue and arouse curiosity;
- to discover what the class already knows about the topic;
- to recall and refresh memories of what has been learned or done previously, prior to explaining the new material or process.

Openings may contain any or all of these ingredients, and teachers need to give careful thought to the topic before deciding which kind of opening to use.

Activity 5

Imagine you are teaching a topic to a class of children who are learning about it for the first time. Plan three different openings that cover each of the following:

- arousing curiosity;
- finding out what children already know *about the topic*;
- using an *advance organiser* to signal what the children are going to learn about.

Look carefully at the three sets of strategies you have chosen. Which would you prefer? Is it possible and/or desirable to combine two or more of your ideas in the same opening?

If you have the opportunity, compare your ideas with those of others in your group.

Intriguing and arousing curiosity

Questioning

Explanations can often have questions asked by teachers and pupils as an integral part of them. The companion volume in the series *Questioning in the Secondary School*, written by the same two authors as this present book, deals with the matter in much greater detail, so we shall not devote as much space to it here as the topic justifies. Within explanations, questioning can serve several purposes. These include:

- to find out what pupils already know, or do not know;
- to shape the line of argument by using pupils' own ideas;
- to check how well pupils understand what is being explained;
- to elicit concrete examples of principles or concepts;
- to help children develop a desire to enquire and learn further, once the explanation is complete.

Different kinds of question can fulfil these various purposes. For example, both closed and open questions can be used to find out what children already know. Suppose a class is studying magnetism, a teacher might ask a closed question, like, 'Does a magnet pick up plastic?' or a more open question such as, 'Can anyone tell me what magnets do and do not pick up?'

The questions can stand alone or may be related to practical work. The teacher might say, 'I've given you twelve different things, like a piece of rubber, a paper clip, a plastic tube, a brass rod, a two-inch nail, and so on. Now I want you to answer two questions. The first is: "Which of these things will the magnet pick up?" Make a guess and then put things you think a magnet will pick up into your *Yes* pile. The second question is: "Which of these things will the magnet *not* pick up?" Put those into your *No* pile. Then I'll give you a magnet and you can see if you're right or not.' The response to these questions would show whether the children already knew some basic principles of magnetism; whether they were completely ignorant and merely assigned the objects randomly; or whether they had a partial understanding, but certain misconceptions, like believing erroneously that magnets attract all metals, instead of just those with iron in them.

Similarly, questions can be used in sequence, either to probe more deeply into an issue, or to take understanding on to higher levels. We return to this topic in Unit 3. Eliciting examples is also a common purpose for questioning ('Can anyone give me an example of a mammal?', 'Who can tell me the name of a shape with right angles in it?').

One of the most challenging kinds of question is the one, often towards the end of an explanatory phase, which poses questions that can only be answered by further study. This is an effective means of motivating pupils to learn after the initial explanation is complete. One teacher we observed concluded her opening phase on 'Diet and Health' by saying, 'So these are some of the things we need to eat to keep ourselves healthy. But we've also talked about food which doesn't do us much good, and might even do us some harm. What I want you to ask yourself is this, "Is the food I eat good for me, or bad for me?" That's why we're all, me included, going to keep a diary of every single thing we eat, and then we'll analyse just how healthy our diet really is.' This personalised question proved a strong motivator as the class went on to study their own food intake over the coming weeks.

Practical work and the use of teaching aids

There are numerous theories about how children learn, some complementary, some contradictory. Amongst the best-known and most cited views are those of Jean Piaget (1954) and Jerome Bruner (1966). Piaget's stages of development posit that some adolescents may still be in the 'concrete operational' stage, capable of logical thinking with concrete things, but not yet able to operate in the abstract, the 'formal operational' stage. Bruner used the terms 'enactive' for the first stage of development when children see objects in terms of what they *do* to or with them, like touch, hold or throw them, and subsequently the 'iconic' stage, when single features, like colour, shape or sound, may dominate children's view of the world. The 'symbolic' stage, when children cope with logic and various symbol systems, comes last.

There has been considerable controversy over the theories of both Piaget and Bruner, but their writings have drawn attention, as have many other writers, including their critics, to the importance of personal practical experience. Abstract concepts can indeed be learned and reproduced mechanically, but even adults who are well able to think in the abstract often welcome concrete examples, or working models. Gardening and cookery programmes on television, for example, would be less popular if they consisted solely of lectures on basic principles, like 'plant nutrition' or 'the application of heat', and never showed real gardens, or actual recipes being made in a kitchen. Similarly, the use by the teacher and/or the pupils of pictures, models, videos, interactive technology, games and posters can enhance learning for those not always able to grasp verbal explanations. Pictures can be used as a stimulus to the imagination, as a means of amplifying a concept, or in their own right. It is not just pupils who are still at Piaget's concrete operational stage who benefit from a good picture or video. A picture of a line of camels in the desert sunlight was used by one teacher as a skilful means of stimulating all the pupils in the class to design a frieze to go around a container. In one video the camera is situated on board a lifeboat which then rotates 360 degrees without sinking, a spectacular adjunct to an explanation of floating.

Other senses can also be brought into play during explanations. A teacher we observed teaching a class about 'friction' asked them to rub their hands together, so that they could feel the heat developing when a force met resistance. Multi-sensory explanations can sometimes be successful when appealing to one single sense, such as hearing or sight, has failed.

Another teacher showed a group of pupils a short exercise on a CD-ROM which enabled them to manipulate a model of the atom, taking it apart, reassembling it and adding particles, with the periodic table available across the screen to explain what they had constructed (e.g. turning a hydrogen atom into a helium atom). This direct involvement manipulating a three-dimensional model on the screen clarified for them the structure of the atom more effectively than his voice and a static model alone.

Practical activities, interactive technology and visual aids, therefore, need to be designed or selected so that they:

- are appropriate to the age and background of the pupils;
- enhance and amplify the concepts, principles or processes being explained;
- involve more than one sense, if this is appropriate;
- are integral to the explanation, not mere adjuncts to it or gimmicks;
- are not confusing and do not confound or cloud the explanation.

Drama and role play

Although teachers of English regularly use drama and role-play as part of their teaching, teachers of other subjects are often more reluctant. Yet many types of explanation would be clearer and better understood if pupils could 'live' them, thereby gaining direct, rather than indirect experience. For example, many modern language teachers use role-play to practise the vocabulary of shopping, travel, or recreation and leisure. A history teacher we observed, instead of launching into a long-winded explanation of the Industrial Revolution, set the pupils an exercise where they had to manufacture shirts (out of paper) and decide whether to invest in machinery (like scissors). Each group then worked out its profits and the teacher subsequently explained the factual information they would need to understand the Industrial Revolution.

This last point is most important. A role-play or game without a proper and conscious link to the facts and principles of what is being studied is a waste of time. This history teacher capitalised on pupils' curiosity and harnessed their direct experience, but he did not use it as a substitute for teaching history, using it rather as a very effective precursor.

The structure of explanations

To some extent the structure of an explanation should help determine its strategies. It is equally arguable, however, that the strategies determine the structure. This paradox depends on teachers' preferred teaching styles and the subject matter. In subjects like mathematics, it is sometimes the case that A must precede B, that unless you can calculate the square of a number and also multiply two numbers, you cannot calculate the area of a circle since this involves both operations. In explanations, therefore, where there is a logical *linear* sequence, it is important to take first things first – that is, to work out the first principles, explain these, and then move on to the next stage.

Not all subject matter falls into this kind of logical sequencing. In history, for example, it might sometimes be essential to sequence the explanation of events in chronological order, but on occasions there is also an argument for a different order. For example, if a class already knows something about the Second World War, it might make sense to start off with a review of what they already know, or do not know, about the events of the 1930s and 1940s, and then move back in time to explore how Hitler enlisted support by exploiting the grievances felt by Germans following the Treaty of Versailles after the First World War.

In many subjects, like science, children can only really construct for themselves the meaning of a key concept when all the parts come together. If they have not understood some elements of an explanation, then it is a like missing sections of a novel: the whole plot can become difficult to follow (Ogborn *et al.*, 1996).

Teachers' personal preferences also enter into the equation. Those who prefer an *a priori rational planning approach* may well want to determine structure in advance. Others who prefer an *intuitive empirical approach* may opt for 'suck-it-and-see', preferring to improvise more in the light of actual pupil response.

When explanations are analysed systematically, a number of features are often detected, and these are discussed more fully in Unit 3. In addition to the *advance organiser* mentioned above, there are often *links* between the central *keys*. Links can often be identified by the prepositions and conjunctions that forge them, words like: because, since, as, in order to, as a result, and so, therefore, by, if … then, the more … the more. Examples of such links are:

> 'People first developed weapons *in order* to defend themselves and also hunt animals for food.'

> '*If* you increase the size *then* you also increase the weight.'

> '*The more* water you put into that paint *the more* messy it is.'

'You can stay in at playtime, *since* you can't behave yourself.'

'You can change the note on the recorder *by* putting your finger over the hole.'

Sometimes the structure of a certain part of an explanation may benefit from a mixture of approaches, provided they are coherent and not random. One frequently used mini-structure of this kind is to combine rules (or principles) and examples, often in the order:

rule – example(s) – rule

as in this instance:

> Modern materials have often been developed to suit the particular purpose they're being used for. Teflon is an example of the coating you put on a pan if you don't want food to stick to it. Fibre optics are used in medicine to explore the inner workings of the human body. Because they're very thin they don't damage you inside as much as a thick rod or a knife would. So you need to look at your problem, or what it is you're trying to achieve or design, and then decide what materials best suit your purpose.

Revision, review, summary and closure

At the end of a lesson, a unit, or even of a relatively short explanation, teachers can employ numerous ways to ensure that pupils understand what has been explained. The summary may be entirely by the *teacher*:

T: Now let's see what we've learned. We've found out that magnets only pick up things with iron in them. Some people thought they picked up all metals, but they didn't attract brass, aluminium, copper or lead when we tried them out. And they only picked up the tin can lid because it's got some iron in it.

It may, alternatively, be by the *pupils*:

T: Who'd like to sum up what we've just been discussing about the mass media?
P: Some of it is broadcast and some of it is in print.
P: People are often trying to persuade you to their point of view.
P: We need to look out for what is true and what is made up.
P: There's good and bad. Just because a newspaper sells a lot of copies, or a television programme has a lot of viewers, doesn't mean to say it must be good.
P: Or bad. It might be well written or well acted. You have to make your own mind up about what is good and bad. Other people can't do it for you.

It can also be by the *teachers and the pupils jointly*, with the teacher 'shaping' the summary:

T: So what does the story tell us about the old man?
P 1: That he's tired.
T: Yes, that's right, but there was more to it than that.
P 2: He's lived a busy life and he's not afraid of dying.
T: And why wasn't he afraid of dying?
P 3: Because he's religious and he believes there's life after death.

Activity 6

Choose an activity in your subject that you are likely to be teaching shortly and think through the following:

How you will introduce it.

What words or phrases, technical, specific to the subject, or part of everyday language, might need explaining.

What feelings or emotions might need exploring and/or explaining.

Who will take responsibility for what.

What, if any, activities might be part of it, and what the sequence might be.

How the session might conclude.

Unit 3   Analysing explanations

During the hundreds of exchanges that most teachers have with their pupils every single day of their teaching career, they may give information, ask questions, praise or reprimand, listen to someone, settle a dispute, hear pupils' accounts of what they are doing and talk socially with an individual or group. Events such as explanations, which happen with great frequency, are well worth analysing in a deliberate and systematic way, for teachers can often slip into set ways of interacting with their pupils. After countless repeats and rehearsals, favoured strategies then become like an old pair of gloves or slippers, so warm and well fitting that one is reluctant to change or discard them, even if they are worn out.

There are numerous ways of analysing explanations, just as there are several approaches to the analysis of classroom events, and many of these are described in the book *An Introduction to Classroom Observation* (Wragg, 1999). It is possible to use both *quantitative* methods, whereby certain aspects of teaching are looked for and tallied when they occur, and *qualitative* forms of analysis, which involve the study of particular events and episodes, the search for meaning, impact or effect and the roles played by participants.

These approaches are different and can be complementary. It is not a question of whether one methodology is intrinsically better than another is, but rather of what is the best approach in the circumstances. Questions like, 'How often?' or 'How much?' may well be answered by an event-counting, quantifying approach. A question like 'What did the pupil understand by …?' may require an incisive case-study approach, since each child is an individual who may or may not react to situations in the same way as others in the same class.

Sometimes we want to know information in quantities – how many pupils were able to solve a particular maths problem and how many got it wrong, for example, so that we know who may need extra help and who is ready to go on to more demanding work. On other occasions it is the unique nature of a problem or situation which is of more concern – why one pupil finds it difficult to understand a particular concept, even if you have tried several different ways of explaining and have given plenty of opportunity for individual practice.

QUANTITATIVE ANALYSIS

In order to see some of the many different ways of analysing explanations, consider this episode from an English lesson. The teacher is explaining about the fictitious 'Island of Zarg', prior to the pupils writing a story about it. A map of the island is in front of each pupil.

> T: Can you see anything that attracts you about the island? Anywhere you'd like to visit, David?
> P1:   Castle Point.
> T: Why would you like to go there?
> P1:   It's exciting.
> T: Yes, it's exciting. Have you found anywhere you'd like to go, Emma?
> P2:   I think …
> T: No, it's Emma's turn. I'd like to hear what Emma has to say.
> P3:   Eastern Moors. There's a creature … it's … it's …
> T: There's something up there that Emma's found. What has she found coming out of the sea?
> P4:   A monster.
> T: Yes, it could be. What's coming out of his hand?
> P2:   Lightning.
> T: What else has he got coming out of him?
> P2:   Rain.
> T: Rain and thunder, so it's almost as if he's in control of the …?
> P2:   Weather.
> T: The weather, yes, I think so … What would be a good word to describe Darkling Forest?
> P3:   Spooky and creepy.
> T: Better than spooky and creepy?
> P3:   Strange and weird.
> T: Yes, strange and weird. How about a word beginning with two 'e's? Do you know it?
> P1:   Eerie.
> T: Yes. What does eerie mean?
> P1:   Scary.

There are many *quantitative* conclusions that one could reach about this short episode, some interesting, some banal. By way of example a few are listed on page 32. Not all quantitative analysis is clear-cut, however, even if it looks precise.

Quantitative information like that given on page 32, standing alone, tells us little about the *quality* of the teaching, about what the pupils have learned, about such important matters as the clarity of the explanation, or, if factual material is involved, the accuracy and correctness of what is being taught. Taken into consideration alongside additional information, however, it can be quite interest-

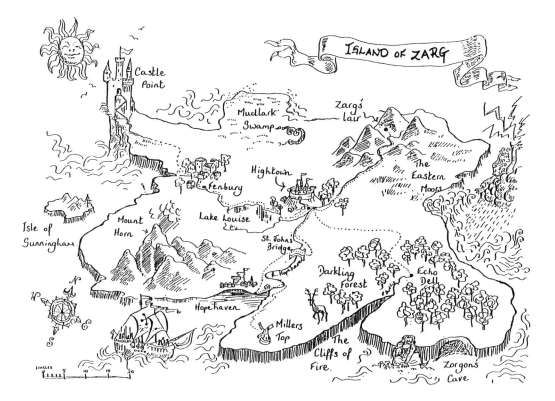

Island of Zarg

ing and valuable, especially when related to other significant information, such as the purposes and intentions of the lesson. For example, suppose the teacher wants to involve several children in the discussion. To get four of them to contribute in about one minute might seem to be not too bad. On the other hand, suppose the teacher really wanted to develop the children's ability not only to write about the island but also to speak confidently and imaginatively, at some length. It might then be disappointing to discover that, in this phase of the lesson at any rate, a typical answer was just one, two or three words long.

QUALITATIVE ANALYSIS

If the principal purpose of the explanation is to bring out salient points about significant features of the island, so that children can compose an imaginative piece of writing, then to some degree the success of the explanation will lie in the extent to which the teacher has broadened their vision and extended their imagination. These are all *qualitative* judgements to do with the nature of what is being learned: what constitutes an 'imaginative' idea or which features are 'significant'. Judgements about the nature of what is being learned, whether something is worthwhile, important, valuable, morally right, in good taste, appropriate to the pupil or group concerned or sufficiently demanding on the

Pupils participating	4	
Teacher's questions	12	
Open questions	7	(approx.)
Closed questions	5	(approx.)
Statements of approval	5	
Statements of disapproval	2	
Reprimands	1	
Length of episode	68	seconds
Total number of words uttered	164	
Words spoken by teacher	138	
Words spoken by pupils	26	
Percentage teacher talk	84	%
Percentage pupil talk	16	%
Length of pauses	19	seconds
Length of talk	49	seconds
Number of teacher utterances	12	
Number of pupil utterances	12	
Percentage of talk	72	%
Percentage of non-talk (pauses, etc.)	28	%
Average length of each teacher utterance	11.5	words
Average length of each pupil utterance	2.17	words
Number of keys (i) Where to visit		
(ii) Why place attracts		
(iii) The nature of the creature		
(iv) The nature of the forest		
Total of 4		
Average length of pause between pupil answer and teacher response	0.6	seconds
Average length of pause between teacher question and pupil response	0.85	seconds

Quantitative analysis of Island of Zarg

intellect, are matters of personal opinion and professional judgement, and cannot be resolved by quantities alone.

It is not possible to say that all closed questions are 'good' or 'bad', just as it was difficult to assign uncontested levels of difficulty to the terms 'higher order' and 'lower order' in the terms of people like Bloom (1956) cited on page 34. It depends on the nature of the thinking involved and the personal judgement someone makes in the circumstances. 'What is the capital of England?' is a not especially demanding closed question. 'What is the formula of DNA?' is also a closed question, in that there is not a choice of answers, but the demands are on a vastly different plane. Similarly, 'Can you tell me the name of something that grows in a garden?' is a more open question requiring little imagination from the respondent, whereas, 'What is the meaning of life?' or 'How could we eradicate poverty in the world?' are open questions of mind-blowing proportions.

A transcript of a lesson cannot give the full flavour of the quality of an explanation. In the episode above, we cannot tell from the text whether the teacher is really cross when saying 'No, it's Emma's turn', or is making the point in a kindly manner. The observer saw it as the latter. We cannot tell, when the teacher asks for words to describe the forest, whether most pupils were thinking about the question and attempting to answer. They were, according to the observer who was present. Nor is it always clear what meanings and significance the teacher or pupils attach to events. This can sometimes be elicited not just by live observation but by interviewing the participants to see how they perceived the process.

The observer of the lesson on page 30 commented on the teacher's and the pupils' enthusiasm, the pleasure the teacher showed at pupils' answers, the generally high level of contribution from the class, the discriminating manner in which the teacher responded to pupils' ideas, and the way that later on, when they began to write, pupils were encouraged to develop their own ideas. The teacher said in interview that she wanted to give them somewhere to start, that that was her main intention: 'They need a starting point. Once they have this, their story can take them anywhere.' When the stories written by this particular group of pupils were scored by two independent markers, as part of the research, they obtained some of the highest scores recorded, compared with other similar groups of pupils with different teachers who were engaged in the same explanation of the same island.

One fruitful way of analysing qualitative aspects of an explanation is to use the *critical events* approach. In order to do this you need to observe someone teaching and to select a period when some kind of explanation is taking place. You then select some event – it need not be spectacular – which seems in your judgement to help or impede children's understanding. This might be a neat analogy, a piece of factually incorrect information, a moment of sudden enlightenment, a well-composed sequence of questions, a failure to clarify someone's confusion, or some other significant happening. Follow the procedures described in Activity 7 on the next page, filling in the spaces.

LEVELS AND TYPES OF THINKING

Explaining is not a one-way process. Unless the pupils actually learn something as a result, the explanation will have been wasted. One common way of analysing explanations from the pupils' point of view is to look at the sort of thinking in which they are being asked to engage. Numerous researchers have designed schedules for such analysis, and not every research instrument is suitable for use by teachers analysing their own lessons. Some are extremely complex and require lengthy training. Others have a focus that might be of limited interest to many teachers, such as those that concentrate on the explanation of scientific concepts.

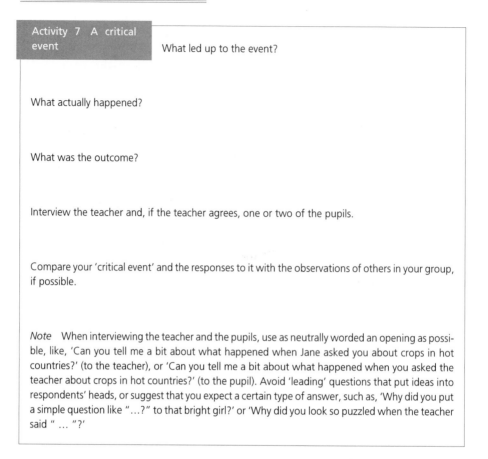

Activity 7   A critical event

What led up to the event?

What actually happened?

What was the outcome?

Interview the teacher and, if the teacher agrees, one or two of the pupils.

Compare your 'critical event' and the responses to it with the observations of others in your group, if possible.

Note   When interviewing the teacher and the pupils, use as neutrally worded an opening as possible, like, 'Can you tell me a bit about what happened when Jane asked you about crops in hot countries?' (to the teacher), or 'Can you tell me a bit about what happened when you asked the teacher about crops in hot countries?' (to the pupil). Avoid 'leading' questions that put ideas into respondents' heads, or suggest that you expect a certain type of answer, such as, 'Why did you put a simple question like "...?" to that bright girl?' or 'Why did you look so puzzled when the teacher said " ... "?'

Many of these approaches have been influenced by Bloom's *Taxonomy of Educational Objectives* (Bloom *et al.*, 1956). Bloom and his colleagues tried to devise a structure that would cover objectives for different levels of thinking, and he described six general categories based on a hierarchical view of thinking in classrooms. Theirs is a hierarchical view, based on logical reasoning rather than any particular theory of learning, and it assumes that higher levels of thought are based on, or make some use of, what is in the lower levels. His six major groupings were, in ascending order of level:

knowledge

comprehension

application

analysis

synthesis

evaluation

"LET ME EXPLAIN THIS SIMPLY:
YOU DO ALL THE WORK.
I COPY IT.
YOU DON'T END UP IN HOSPITAL.."

In order to *comprehend*, it was argued, you must have knowledge. To be able to *synthesise*, you will need to be able to *analyse*.

There have been many modifications of this sort of taxonomic approach, including some that have created extra headings, or evolved more specific sub-headings of the major categories. We and other investigators have often extended the categories of analysis to include such abilities as:

- distinguish fact from opinion;
- distinguish relevant from irrelevant information;
- detect error in thinking;
- infer purposes, points of view, thoughts, feelings;
- recognise bias or propaganda.

One of the most interesting outcomes of that particular view of children's thinking was the work of Hilda Taba and her associates at San Francisco State College (Taba, 1966). She believed that teachers could learn to move children up to higher levels of thinking, provided they knew how to analyse the relevant processes in the classroom. She concentrated, in particular, on the explanation of concepts, and on children knowing how to make inferences and apply principles. Her emphasis was on learning what to focus on, and then embarking on a set of steps that would extend and lift children's thinking, as teachers and children both gave and sought information. Taba's thought levels were as follows:

0   Incorrect information;

1   Specific items of data;

2   Relating, comparing, contrasting items of data;

3   Factual explanation, or factual support of prediction;

4   Inferences from units of data, predictions;

5   Inferential logic;

6   Generalisation from inferences.

Children were encouraged to move up to higher levels as they studied topics like 'The Pioneers'. Thus, a level–1 statement by a child would be, 'Sometimes the wagons got stuck in the snow' (specific item of data). A level–2 piece of thinking, which involved comparing and contrasting, would be 'Well, the pioneers weren't travelling on the ocean, like the colonists, they were travelling on just land.' Higher levels, according to Taba, would be achieved when children were helped to make inferences or generalisations from these. An example she gave of level-5, inferential logic, was, 'I'd rather have been with the colonists, because if I was a pioneer, I'd have had to walk all those miles and I don't think my feet would ever feel the same.' A level–6 statement would be, 'The witch doctors are trying to do with wands and cracked eggs what our doctors do with needles', showing the child making a generalisation from inferences.

The Russian psychologist Lev Vygotsky (1978) highlighted the importance of adults in helping children develop ideas which require mental operations just above what appears to be their current ceiling, in what he called the 'zone of proximal development'. Explaining plays a vital part in liberating children, so that they can eventually perform higher order tasks unaided. Jerome Bruner and his colleagues (Wood, Bruner and Ross, 1976) use the metaphor of 'scaffolding' to describe the structured assistance that adults give to children while their grasp of something is frail. The explaining teacher acts like the scaffolding around a building, at first giving support and then gradually removing it, as pupils begin to understand for themselves what is involved and no longer need external aid.

This attachment of importance of the *learner's* thinking, when topics are being explained, not just to the teacher's efforts, has been developed in different subjects of the curriculum. Adey and Shayer (1994) have worked specifically in the fields of mathematics and science. Their research into teaching children to think like a mathematician or scientist, has led to the *CAME (Cognitive Acceleration through Mathematics Education)* and *CASE (Cognitive Acceleration through*

Science Education) projects. The evidence suggests that pupils who learned this kind of thinking in the early years of secondary school were likely to obtain, on average, one grade higher than they might have scored when they eventually took the General Certificate of Secondary Education.

In another specialist project, *Thinking through Geography* (Leat, 1998), pupils concentrate on learning the key concepts which underpin geographical knowledge. Seeing explanation as a *two-way process*, wherein both explainer and learner have to engage, seems to pay dividends. Many teachers have an intuitive belief, even if it is not always easy for them to prove empirically, that it is *desirable* for children to learn to think in different ways, some of which are arguably on a 'higher' plane than recalling facts alone. It is a topic, therefore, that is worthy of some careful scrutiny.

PUPILS EXPLAINING

If explaining is a two-way process, not solely a means for teachers to give something to pupils, then there will be many examples of interactive explanations, and not just between teacher and pupils. Children often can and do explain things to one another in class and at home. It is quite common for young pupils to say that their elder brother or sister helps them at home if they are stuck on their homework, and inside the classroom it is a regular occurrence for pupils to quiz each other when they need assistance. Many children are able to empathise with a fellow learner at a similar stage and use the right language or examples to make the point clearly, though one should not pretend that it is always like this.

It is well worth the time and effort involved to encourage members of the class, from the first time you take them, to teach one another. Learning to explain a concept to another pupil serves two important functions. The first is that the child practises clear communication and thinks about the audience, even if this is only one person; the second is that explaining to someone else can often clarify your own ideas, or reveal what it is that you do not yourself fully understand. There are many examples of a pupil trying to explain something to another pupil and then calling in the teacher to help clarify a particular point, as in the following exchange between two pupils, one showing the other how to make a small kite out of wood veneer strip and tissue paper:

P 1: You have to glue these two strips together no [pointing to two strips of wood veneer] not like that – in a cross shape.

P 2: Where's the glue?

P 1: Trevor's got it. Don't get it on the tissue paper or it won't fly.

P 2: How long does this strip have to be?

P 1: You put one strip downwards and then the other strip across it, like a cross.

P 2: Yes, but what if you put two of the same together, what if this across piece is the same length as the down bit, will it still fly? I bet it'll crash.

P 1: I'll ask miss. Miss! What happens if these two bits of wood are the same length? Will it crash?

Activity 8

Give members of your class the opportunity to explain something to one another. Set up an activity where you explain something to one member of a pair or a group, who must then, in turn, explain it to the others. It could be a simple piece of gymnastics in a PE lesson, instructions on how to do a maths problem, or a design and technology activity like designing and making something.

Eavesdrop discreetly on some of the 'explanations' as they occur around the room.

Make brief notes under the following headings:

Clarity   (Is the explanation generally clear to the other pupil(s)?)

Language   (Does the explainer use appropriate language?)

Examples   (Does the pupil give an example or demonstration?)

Organisation   (Bearing in mind the age of the child, is it well organised?)

Learning   (Do both explainer and other(s) appear to have learned something?)

Discuss your findings with the pupils concerned and, in a sensitive manner, with the class. What can you do to improve the children's skill at explaining?

USING SCHEDULES

Many teachers prefer to analyse their own thinking by reflecting on it, rather than by writing notes. Sometimes, however, it can be useful to have a written account of an explanation, either a self-critique or a set of notes compiled by an observer. This can be particularly useful for initial trainees, when tutors and supervising teachers can offer the student a written version of their analysis. It can also be valuable during the classroom observation parts of teacher appraisal. If the emphasis of lesson analysis is to improve the quality of teaching, then a written account can be a positive step towards this goal.

Often a freehand account is preferable, as the observer can react to events as they occur and then, after the lesson, discuss any notes that have been made, leaving a copy for the teacher's own use. Sometimes people prefer more structure and may find a rating schedule, or a lesson observation pro-forma, more helpful. Rating schedules must be used with care. They are best employed by experienced observers who have seen many teachers at work and have some idea of the range of skills to be seen in many primary classrooms. Often five -or seven-point scales are featured with 1 indicating 'weak' and 5 or 7 meaning 'excellent'. A typical rating schedule for analysing and commenting on explanations in a lesson or series of lessons, might look like this:

Typical rating schedule for analysing explanations

Circle the appropriate number: 7 represents 'truly outstanding' teaching,
1 indicates 'a weak point', 4 is average for someone with your experience.

Explanations

1 Your explanations were clearly understood by the pupils.	1 2 3 4 5 6 7
2 Your explanations covered the essential points.	1 2 3 4 5 6 7
3 The examples, analogies and illustrations you gave were appropriate.	1 2 3 4 5 6 7
4 You listened to children's responses.	1 2 3 4 5 6 7
5 You clarified children's responses where necessary.	1 2 3 4 5 6 7
6 You made effective use of teaching aids where appropriate.	1 2 3 4 5 6 7
7 You made effective use of your voice.	1 2 3 4 5 6 7

Usually such a schedule would also contain a 'Comments' section, enabling the observer to make specific remarks about, for example, factual accuracy and the quality of demonstrations, if these were appropriate, and such matters as movement or gesture, where these amplified explanations.

Sometimes a more sharply focused schedule or outline is helpful if you want to concentrate on analysing and improving a particular aspect of explaining. Suppose, for example, you wanted to improve the clarity of your explanation by making the central keys or ideas more distinct and effectively linked. In that case, a format like the one on page 41 might be helpful. The teacher enters the keys or main ideas in the centre boxes before the lesson, and the observer then makes notes about the teacher's and pupils' use of language in the left-hand and right-hand boxes.

Sometimes it is helpful, with certain explanations, to draw a diagram showing what the key ideas will be and how they will relate and be linked. This can be done both by the teacher *before* the lesson and by the observer *during* the lesson, to see how the links work out in practice.

Another approach is to use a scale of frequency, like 'always/usually/sometimes/once/never'. This would only give a frequency of events, in itself relatively limited, so a qualitative comment section is essential, otherwise the categories could be too restricted. An example of this approach is shown in Activity 9, which is a paired activity. Two teachers, two students, or a student and a teacher working reciprocally can do it, each observing the other in turn.

Activity 9

Use the observation schedule on page 40 in another teacher's or student's lessons.

Ask the other person to observe you using the same observation schedule.

Discuss each other's lessons and both your observations.

Consider how you can improve your own explaining skill.

	Always	Usually	Sometimes	Once	Never	Comments
Clear introduction	☐	☐	☐	☐	☐	
New term clarified	☐	☐	☐	☐	☐	
Apt word choice	☐	☐	☐	☐	☐	
Clear sentence structure	☐	☐	☐	☐	☐	
Vagueness avoided	☐	☐	☐	☐	☐	
Adequate concrete examples	☐	☐	☐	☐	☐	
Within pupils' experience	☐	☐	☐	☐	☐	
Voice used to emphasise	☐	☐	☐	☐	☐	
Emphasis by gestures	☐	☐	☐	☐	☐	
Appropriate pauses	☐	☐	☐	☐	☐	
Direct verbal cueing	☐	☐	☐	☐	☐	
Repetition used	☐	☐	☐	☐	☐	
Main ideas paraphrased	☐	☐	☐	☐	☐	
Sound use of media, materials	☐	☐	☐	☐	☐	
Pattern of explanation clear	☐	☐	☐	☐	☐	
Parts linked to each other	☐	☐	☐	☐	☐	
Progressive summary	☐	☐	☐	☐	☐	
Pace or level altered	☐	☐	☐	☐	☐	
Opportunity for pupil questions	☐	☐	☐	☐	☐	
Grasp of main ideas checked	☐	☐	☐	☐	☐	
Pupil commitment sought	☐	☐	☐	☐	☐	

Note to observer: tick whichever box you judge as appropriate in each case. Some aspects will not be seen often, and your comments will clarify the category chosen.

Observation schedule for explaining

Format for analysis of key ideas in explanation

Observer's notes on features of teacher's language use	*Ideas or 'keys' being explained (to be filled in by the teacher before the lesson)*	*Observer's notes on features of pupil's language use*

Unit 4   Knowing the subject matter

Throughout the world knowledge is being produced at a phenomenal rate in every conceivable subject. Teachers are the bearers of social genes in our fast-moving society, able to transmit knowledge, skills, values and culture to future generations. In order to carry out this task successfully, particularly when passing on a concept or an idea, their own knowledge of the relevant subject matter must be accurate and correct. There is no point in being a brilliant exponent of the art of explaining and then filling children's heads with incorrect information and dreary ideas, or equipping them with low-level skills when they and their pupils are capable of achieving something better.

MASTERING SUBJECT MATTER

The professional expertise of people who have become masters of different kinds of subject matter can consist of many elements. Mastery involves more than the mere mechanical acquisition of certain factual information, though having a formidable body of knowledge is a central requisite. Those who have mastered a particular subject or profession will usually have acquired:

- a significant body of knowledge;
- an understanding of the major and many minor concepts central to the subjects;
- an understanding of the structure of the subject and a desire to learn more about it.

Take a subject like music as an example. Professional musicians will have a considerable grasp of, usually, a wide range of musical knowledge, from simple concepts of notation up to an intimate knowledge of numerous symphonies, concertos, operas, songs and other types of music. They will have the skill to play certain instruments at a very high standard of proficiency, or to sing, to compose, to conduct, to score and to improvise. They will also usually have a lifelong interest in music that leads them to broaden and extend their repertoire, improve their playing or singing, or create new compositions, throughout their career. There is even some evidence to suggest that, in the case of those musicians who use their fingers, for example, the parts of their brain that control fingering will develop greater capacity and that this may be related to the amount of practice they have done (Howe, 1999).

The subject demands on secondary teachers are now formidable, no matter what subject they teach. Modern linguists are expected to be right up to date with contemporary spoken and written language, able to cover non-fiction as well as traditional fiction. Science specialists are expected to know about both physical and biological sciences, earth science, technology, meteorology and astronomy. Since their classes may have watched television programmes on any conceivable scientific topic, from polymers to genetic modification, they may also be asked questions about topics about which they know less than their better-informed pupils.

Even very young children will have seen spectacular films about their environment. One of the authors of this book was once teaching a class of 6- and 7-year-olds. The topic was 'The World Around Us' and pupils were invited to ask questions about their own immediate environment. In the first 30 seconds this group of children of modest ability asked, 'Why are cars made of metal?', 'Why does smoke come out of the back of a motor bike?', 'Why does it snow?' and 'Why does a wagtail wag its tail?' It was nothing that a couple of lifetimes in the nearest multimedia library could not have solved, but most of us are as competent to handle the more searching questions asked by children as to perform a piece of triple bypass surgery.

Knowledge of subject matter and strategies for explaining are often closely connected. If you have a good grasp of the content (i.e. *what* is to be taught), it puts you in a better position to determine appropriate strategies (i.e. *how* to explain the topic), though mastery of subject matter does not actually guarantee clear exposition. Some knowledgeable people, paralysed by the complexity of what they know, are not able to communicate and empathise with those in possession of less knowledge. Not every Nobel prize-winner would be able to instruct a group of 13-year-olds, though some are brilliant explainers of their knowledge.

Different topics involve different kinds of subject matter. In order to explain to a class how to use a microelectronics kit, why certain materials are better than others when designing and constructing something, the causes and course of the Civil War, how to calculate the volume of a three-dimensional shape, or what erosion is, teachers need to possess, or have access to, considerable bodies of the relevant subject matter. Explaining about the quality of writing in a book, the finer points of citizenship in the twenty-first century, how people deal with moral dilemmas, the impact on the emotions of a poem, painting, piece of music, or the spirit in which team games should be played, involves a mixture of factual content, judgements about values, the intelligence of feeling and a degree of imagination.

Explanations, where part of the 'subject matter' requires use of the imagination, pose an interesting problem. If the teacher prescribes too much in advance, then both children's and teachers' imagination could be inhibited. Yet a certain amount of explaining and exploring must take place.

Activity 10

The following exercise is worth doing even if you are not a teacher of English, citizenship, or personal, social and health education. It is an interesting idea to use during tutor group time, for example, and gives insights into aspects of children's learning that might not always be apparent during lessons in your main subjects.

1   Plan a lesson for a group of pupils in which you will explore ideas with them on a topic of general interest prior to their doing a piece of writing. For example, the topic could be: why do girls often do better than boys at school? Work out what information/resources they may need (e.g. information about test scores at the age of eleven for boys and girls, nationally and within the school; gender, social and cultural issues).

2   Explore the topic interactively with the class and then ask them to write their own account of the issue. Make a tape- or video-recording of the lesson, if possible.

3   Read and mark the class's written work and discuss it with them.

4   Consider the following questions:

   (a)   *What was the nature and structure of your lesson?*

      How did you introduce the topic?

      What seemed to be the main ideas or keys: statistical evidence, like test results; pupils' feelings and beliefs about gender differences; creating a sense of enquiry about the nature of different subjects, the functioning of the human brain and whether boys' brains worked differently from girls' brains; exploration of prejudices and comparison with such 'facts' as exist; excitement; exploiting curiosity; considering the future of employment? How did these evolve? Were they linked?

   (b)   *What strategies did you employ?*

      What did you *tell* the class?

      What sort of *questions* did you ask?

      What additional *aids* did you use – tables? pictures? anecdotes or stories?

      Did you use any other approaches, like drama or role play?

   (c)   *What did members of the class do?*

      Were they active or passive?

      How did they respond to the main ideas and keys?

      What did they initiate themselves?

      How did their contributions and ideas affect the development of the lesson?

   (d)   *What was the written work like?*

      Did it appear to have been influenced by the activities that preceded it? If so, in what way? If not, why not?

      Was the written response what you expected?

      What particularly pleased you? What disappointed you?

      What did the pupils say to you about the activity and their own writing?

      Did they seem to have found it an interesting and absorbing assignment?

(e)   *How did you assess their writing?*

What features of the writing did you particularly value? Factual accuracy? Argument? Use of evidence?

What did you do about spelling, punctuation, grammatical or syntactical errors?

What sort of explaining did you do when you handed the work back?

5   In the light of your experience of teaching the lesson, of listening to and viewing it on tape, and, if you had the opportunity, of discussing it with the class, and with an observer if that was possible, of reading the pupils' writing, and reflecting on the whole exercise, how would you improve what you did? See if you can do a similar activity with the group and then compare the two. Was your second effort more effective?

EXPLAINING CONCEPTS

Learning subject matter often involves mastering a set of concepts. These can be of several kinds. Some of the salient concepts can be said to be the 'keys' which, when linked, lead to understanding. Like pieces in a jigsaw puzzle, if you put them together in the right way and you may have a picture of the whole thing. Some concepts are tiny and precise, others are large and diffuse, open to different interpretations. The concept 'happiness', for example, may have quite different features in the eyes of an Inuit Eskimo, a child, a millionaire and a Trappist monk, but what is in common is that their individual versions of it give them pleasure or satisfaction.

There are four essential features that need to be considered when explaining concepts. These are:

1   *Label or name*   The actual word(s) used to name the concept – 'crops', 'reptile', 'electricity', 'harmony', 'colour', 'monarchy', 'ambition'.

2   *Attributes*   These are of two kinds:

(a)   *must have* – features which are essential parts of the concept, indeed, that are criteria for its definition, such as 'wings' (bird), 'having a grandchild' (grandparents), 'eagerness to succeed' (ambition);

(b)   *may have* – features which occur in certain cases, but are not prerequisites, such as 'brown coloured' birds (applies to sparrows and thrushes, but not to every bird), 'retired' grandparents (many are still working), 'seeking wealth' in ambitious people (some may seek power and scorn wealth).

3   *Examples*   These are also of two kinds:

(a)   *illustrative examples* – actual cases which meet the criteria, such as 'robin' (bird), 'Mr and Mrs Scroggins' (grandparents), 'seeking out influential people to further one's career' (ambition);

(b)   *not-examples* – cases which do not meet the criteria, but then, by comparison, illustrate what the real criteria for inclusion in the concept actually are, such as 'dragon-fly' (flies, but is not a bird), 'Mr and Mrs Bloggs' (elderly, but not grandparents), 'obtaining promotion' (often the result of ambition, but could also happen to the unambitious).

4   *Rules*   The full definition listing the 'must have' attributes and their relationship to each other.

If we were to map out the familiar concept 'Insects' according to this scheme, it would look like this:

Subject area	Science (*subdivisions* – biology – zoology)
Name	Insect
Attributes	(i) *must have* – six legs, head, thorax, abdomen, two antennae, wings; (ii) *may have* – a woodland habitat, a black or brown body, stripes, a beautiful appearance, a liking for fruit, a smooth shell, hairy legs.
Examples	(i) *illustrative examples* – house-fly, beetle, butterfly, wasp, ladybird (ii) *not-examples* – spider (arachnid), scorpion (arachnid), snail (gastropod), woodlouse (isopod land crustacean).
Rules	Insects have six legs, a head, thorax and abdomen, two antennae and two or four wings.

Another valuable use of 'not-examples' is to clarify what the true attributes of the concept are. By comparing a honeycomb, a chessboard or a crossword puzzle where the shapes do 'tessellate' – that is, fit together in a regular pattern – with what happens when you try to press differently sized circles or most star shapes together, where they will not meet all round, the concept of 'tessellation' becomes clearer.

Looking at the 'not-examples' and 'may have' attributes can also help avoid stereotyping, as well as aid the development of more rigorous thinking in children. Stereotyping is often wrong and crude, but its origins lie in it being, on occasion, a biological lifesaver. If we stay well away from all snakes, simply because some are poisonous, then this will help us avoid being bitten by those that are venomous. Stereotyping is the acquisition of a fixed mental attitude to something on the basis of one or more characteristics.

Unfortunately it is also an oversimplification that is sometimes, indeed can often be, incorrect, even though it is related to accommodating the environment in order to survive. In childhood, for example, most of us are at some time stung by a bee or a wasp. We then stereotype all black-and-yellow striped insects as likely to sting and therefore to be avoided, yet many are completely harmless and enjoy, as a result of their colouring, some immunity from predators. If a teacher were explaining the concept 'Ruritanian', then the only definition of it may be 'those born in, or naturalised as residents of, Ruritania'. But if children have met or read about a Ruritanian who is lazy, violent or dishonest, they may generalise this 'may have' attribute to all Ruritanians and wrongly stereotype them.

Activity 11

1   Choose two key concepts which you are likely to need to explain to a class, a group or an individual. Select one which is fairly specific and definable, like 'mammal', 'island', or 'the Romans', and one which is more diffuse and difficult to pin down, such as 'progress', 'a good building', or 'great music/art'.

2   Map out each of the two according to the scheme suggested above with attributes, examples and rules.

3   Explain the concept to a group of pupils, or even to an individual. See what strategies and teaching aids you need to make the concept clear – a video of a current affairs programme or part of a debate in Parliament? A drawing or photograph of an island or a map? Pictures of various buildings? A tape of different kinds of music or a collection of different styles of painting, so the group can discuss what constitutes 'great' music or art?

4   Evaluate to what extent your 'map' of the concept helped in the exposition of it.

WRITTEN EXPLANATIONS

Teachers are not the sole sources of information available to pupils. In addition to pictures, videos, tapes, various forms of interactive technology, television and radio, there is a wide variety of print material – books, worksheets, pamphlets, newspapers, magazines and the printed word parts of pictures or diagrams. Many of the acts of explaining in which teachers find themselves engaged are related to printed text – a worksheet, perhaps – which has been compiled by the teacher, or a textbook published commercially.

Much of what has been learned about explanations in textbooks is of relevance to what is covered in this book. Explanations of critical subject matter and key concepts can be clouded, both in textbooks and classroom teaching, by such factors as lack of clarity, inappropriate language, poor links between ideas, or inaccuracy. In some cases it may be the presence of only one or two technical words or phrases which make a text difficult, and teachers might have to explain these so that their pupils can cope with a text which otherwise may not be too difficult for them.

Activity 12

1   Read this passage and then answer the questions below:

Timefrittoons

Most people have at least one timefrittoon. Many of us have several and some people acquire more as they get older. Erdgraben is a common timefrittoon, and it can be quite geldverlangend, though older people often have to make it ungeldverlangend. One elderly man devotes every single day to his timefrittoon. He doesn't mind that erdgraben can be a dirty timefrittoon. 'I don't find it very geldverlangend at all,' he said recently, 'my cousin's timefrittoon is quite a bit more geldverlangend than mine and nowhere near as healthy.'

(a)   Give the names of three timefrittoons.

(b)   Which is likely to be the most geldverlangend?

(c)   Can erdgraben sometimes be a dirty timefrittoon?

(d)   Are all dogs healthy?

(e)   Write a short essay on 'Timefrittoons in the Twenty-first Century'.

2   What do you think the passage is about? How well did you answer the questions? You were probably able to answer some of them without even understanding the passage. For example, you could answer (a) in part, because the text tells you that erdgraben is a timefrittoon; the answer to (c) is also given in the passage, because erdgraben can be dirty; you could have answered (d) without even reading the passage, because it is quite clear that all dogs are not healthy (the mention of dogs is a distracter, it has nothing to do with the passage) and you may have been able to waffle on in the essay in (e) with a bit of deft footwork. Answers to questions that appear on the surface to be 'correct' do not always guarantee understanding.

3   If you were a pupil, you would probably want your teacher to explain three unfamiliar terms to you – *timefrittoon*, *erdgraben* and *geldverlangend/ungeldverlangend* – so that you could understand the passage properly. So now read the text again, in the knowledge that:

timefrittoons are 'hobbies',

erdgraben is 'gardening'

geldverlangend/ungeldverlangend is 'expensive/inexpensive'.

4   Take a textbook or worksheet you are using with a group of pupils and identify any words or phrases that you think might cause them difficulties. Ask some of the pupils to tell you which terms they do not understand. Are your lists the same? Try explaining the terms to the pupils. Read some of the work on text readability (Harrison, 1996).

COPING STRATEGIES

Even well-informed teachers can be caught out by pupils' tricky questions. We have conducted a number of studies of teachers' own subject knowledge and the gaps in it. Even within a field like science there can be wide differences between teachers, depending on whether their major strengths lie in the physical or biological sciences. History teachers may have to cover thousands of years of history in many different lands and cultures, so they too will have gaps in their knowledge. Learning to cope with this, rather than becoming a bluffer, or turning into one of those teachers who covers ignorance by reprimanding the pupil for daring to ask the question, involves the development of coping strategies.

One of the most difficult problems is coping with unpredicted events or with pupils' spontaneous questions. When asked why an orange floats with its peel on, but sinks when peeled, or why most sand sinks, but some grains stay on the surface, teachers would be bereft if they did not have the necessary grasp of such concepts as 'density', 'surface tension' or 'Archimedes' Principle', all of which may be necessary for an explanation of certain kinds of the phenomena associated with floating and sinking.

Using websites judiciously

Teachers use various strategies for coping with their own lack of knowledge, including frank admission (one primary teacher began a lesson on electrical circuits with, 'Look, I have to be honest with you. I know nothing about electricity. I can just about change a fuse'), occasionally evasion, sometimes an offer to find out, or an invitation to the pupils to investigate for themselves.

There are several reasons why teachers need to learn to devise strategies for when they are explaining unfamiliar subject matter. There could be a safety issue (gymnastics and contact sports like rugby, the use of tools, especially those that are electrically powered or that cut); teachers who appear to know too little about their subject will eventually lose respect and continued personal growth is an important part of teachers' professional development.

Lack of sound subject knowledge can also affect teaching strategies. For example, if you didn't know what a capacitor is, in a lesson about microelectronics, you would neither give a convincing explanation, nor be able to think up an appropriate analogy, like, 'A capacitor introduces a delay in the circuit, so when you switch on, the bulb won't light up immediately. There will be a short delay with a small capacitor and a longer delay with a big capacitor. It's a bit like a bucket filling up with water. A little bucket will soon fill up and then overflow, but a bigger bucket will take longer.'

Most of the teachers we have interviewed said they wanted *people* to help them if they were stuck. Some used another specialist, like their head of department (it was particularly embarrassing when heads of department had to consult younger and more recently qualified colleagues!). Others used some kind of centre, like a university or specialist library. Many people use the internet, though this can be hazardous, because there is not the same degree of control over what appears on the internet as there is over what is written in a book, so thousands of erroneous pieces of information appear on web sites and this is a real pitfall for pupils as well as teachers. Some teachers preferred asking a friend, sometimes a spouse, or a school governor who happens to be an expert, especially about cultural and religious matters in multicultural schools. One teacher even used a parent who was a science graduate. Think of the following possibilities, in your own case, should you find yourself on unfamiliar ground:

- *People who can help*   a fellow teacher, a friend, someone on a 'help' line, a librarian, an adviser;
- *Books*   encyclopaedias, library sources, dictionaries, specialist texts;
- *Multimedia*   videos, tapes, pictures, interactive technology, the internet, broadcast radio and television.

Finally, reflect on these strategies and consider how you would react if they were to occur in your classroom.

- You could avoid the issue (not fair, if you can manage to help, you should);
- you might ask the pupil to find out for him- or herself (but help is needed: a suggestion of a book, dictionary or source of information like the library or a database);
- you could promise to find out for another day (but you need to honour this promise, otherwise children feel let down);
- you might ask a group of people to find out (but again, help is needed – who does what? and where?);
- you could try to find out jointly with the class ('I'll write to X, you write to Y').

Activity 13

1   Ask a class to write down questions about concepts, issues, skills, ideas in your subject that they find difficult or do not grasp.

2   Read the questions through privately and decide how you will explain them.

3   Ask yourself which are the easy and which are the hard questions and why?

4   How do you explain the hard questions? What strategies do you use?

5   What do you do if you are confronted with questions about which your own knowledge is not entirely secure?

Unit 5 Effective explaining

Words like 'effective', 'skilful' and 'successful' are not always easy to justify, even if they trip lightly off the tongue. There are teachers who are well liked by pupils, there are those whose classes do well in formal tests, there are many who are admired by their superiors or by their colleagues and there are those who are given high ratings by external assessors and inspectors. They are not necessarily the same teachers. It is possible to be 'effective' on one set of criteria, but not on another.

For some people, effectiveness means carrying out whatever the teacher intended to carry out, so pupils should be given a test, whereby 'success' is judged according to how well they score. But critics of this approach say that tests measure only a limited amount of what has been learned. Consequently, judgements about effectiveness are often made on the basis of several sources of information, on some kind of consensus. These indicators can include test scores; other assessments of pupil learning; professional judgement by someone competent to appraise classroom teaching; self-appraisal by the teacher; opinions of others thought to be competent to judge, such as heads of schools, fellow teachers and pupils themselves. In practice, it is not usually possible, or even desirable, to subject a teacher to all these forms of review at once. In this unit, therefore, we shall concentrate on pupil learning, self-appraisal, classroom strategies, and some of the research on effective explaining. We begin by reviewing some of the points made earlier in this book.

MAIN FEATURES OF EFFECTIVE EXPLAINING

Clarity

Nate Gage (1968) put this in a nutshell:

> Some people explain aptly, getting to the heart of the matter with just the right terminology, examples and organisation of ideas. Other explainers,

the contrary, get us and themselves all mixed up, use terms beyond our ʳel of comprehension, draw inept analogies.

ɪ, therefore, includes some of the following features:

Clear structure

The *'keys'* or central ideas are distinct and the essence of them, attributes, concepts, whatever, is made clear. There are links between the main ideas and these give the whole explanation coherence and a logical shape. There is a clearly set out opening and, where necessary, a closing review or summary from the teacher, the pupils or book.

Clear language

The choice of words and phrases are apt for both the topic and the child or children concerned, being neither too banal, nor at too high a level of abstraction. In other words, the linguistic *register* is appropriate and the words are well chosen.

Clear voice

The voice is well modulated with light and shade, not pitched at a fixed level of monotony. The voice is amplified by gesture and movement, emphasis, facial expression and animation, as is suitable in the circumstances.

Fluency

Clarity can be maintained and indeed enhanced by fluency. The explanation flows at the sort of pace that holds the attention, rather than allows a lapse into tedium. Genuine enthusiasm and interest by the teacher can help stimulate flow.

Strategies

Since explaining is not a one-way process, nor merely a question of someone who knows something drilling it into the head of someone who does not, a wide range of strategies may be effective. These include the following:

1   *Questioning*   Using appropriate questions to see how much pupils already know, to discover what they understand, to review what they have learned, to reflect the higher- or lower-order of thinking which is necessary.

2   *Use of examples/analogies*   Choosing or eliciting illustrative examples and 'not-examples', analogies and 'not-analogies', anecdotes or stories, appropriate to the level of intellectual development of the child or group.

3   *Use of practical work*   Selection or endorsement (if ideas come from pupils) of practical work and activities which enhance understanding.

4   *Use of teaching aids*   Using a range of pictorial or other materials, interactive technology, images and sounds that involve several of the senses, to reinforce or amplify the explanatory process, varying the stimulus sensitively.

5   *Management/organisation*   Arranging discussion, activities, movement and seating so that optimum conditions for learning and understanding are established and a high degree of attentiveness and involvement is maintained. Such matters as these and notions like 'eye contact' and 'vigilance' are covered in the book *Class Management in the Secondary School* in this series.

THE PUPIL'S PERSPECTIVE

The principal purpose of an explanation is to give understanding to the learner, though it may, at the same time, clarify matters for the teacher. This aspect highlights several points that are relevant when the effectiveness of explaining is appraised. Indeed, the ability to *empathise* with the learner is the hallmark of the effective explainer. The ability to see concepts, issues and processes from the learner's point of view means that the choice of language, examples, points to emphasise, review questions and so on, will be more apt.

A simple example is in the use of gesture. If you are explaining a set of figures in a graph that show a *downward* trend, and if your audience is facing you, you would need to move your finger from high right to low left (Picture A on page 56) as *you* see it, so that it comes over to *them* as high left to low right (Picture B on page 56). If you demonstrate the trend line from your own point of view, the class will see the movement the wrong way round. This is a banal example of empathy, perhaps, but it illustrates the principle of seeing what you are explaining from someone else's viewpoint.

Points to be borne in mind when talking of the pupil's perspective include:

1   *Understanding*   During the explanatory process, pupils' understanding should be growing and the teacher should be able to predict roughly the final expected level of attainment, given the capabilities of the child or group concerned.

2   *Involvement*   Pupils themselves need to be involved in the process, rather than merely act as the passive recipients of an explanation, i.e. participating in discussion, asking and answering questions, making suggestions or observations and helping to shape the process, wherever this is appropriate. This is not to say that every explanation should be interactive, but that there should be sensitivity to the active role that members of the class might play.

3   *Mutual explanation*   Opportunities should be provided for pupils to explain to teachers, and also for pupils to explain to one another.

As the teacher sees it (Picture A)

As the children see it (Picture B)

4   *Listening*   Teachers must listen to their pupils and respond to what they hear, while pupils must listen to the teacher and to one another. People sometimes say that they are listening, but they have often already decided what they are going to do next, or they think they know what pupils are going to say, so they 'listen' with closed ears.

5   *Using and extending ideas*   It is important to secure some degree of involvement, but a further step is to weave pupils' ideas into the discussion or activity and then extend these. One teacher of pupils with special needs we observed regularly built his explanations around pupils' proposals: 'Now Ian says that these two cars won't run as far on this rough cloth, but Gemma thinks it won't make any difference, so let's see what happens …'

6   *Humour*   There are many kinds of humour, and studies have shown that children like humour, although they dislike sarcasm. Humour related to the concept(s) being explained (as opposed to gratuitously humorous asides not relevant to the topic), may help learning, since it can aid recall and, in certain cases, enhance understanding. Humour should appear natural and spontaneous because forced humour can have a much less positive effect.

7   *Further appetite*   Try to create a feeling that something interesting and worthwhile has been learned and thus whet pupils' appetite for learning more.

DISCOVER OR BE TOLD?

Many issues in education become over-simplified and are often portrayed as consisting of polar opposites – 'good' versus 'bad' – when people's practices are much more diverse. One of the most frequent issues is about discovery learning and didactic teaching, where the emphasis in the former is on children finding out for themselves, and in the latter on teachers telling their pupils. Within the teaching profession there is much more tolerance of diversity than outside it. Most teachers recognise that it is common practice to vary one's strategies and styles according to circumstances, so that a teacher may give information directly on one occasion and encourage children to explore a topic on another.

Often in the mass media, however, the assumption is that teachers are in two fiercely opposed camps: 'traditional' and 'progressive'. Yet in the fifth century BC, Confucius described in his *Analects* how he capitalised on the urge to discover: 'If out of the four corners of a subject I have dealt thoroughly with one corner and the pupils cannot then find out the other three for themselves, then I do not explain any more.'

Discovery, related as it is to the satisfying of curiosity – a powerful drive in children – can be highly motivating. When young children learn for the first time that a magnet will pick up a paper clip, and that the paper clip will in turn, now that it is magnetised, pick up a second paper clip, they can be beside themselves with excitement. If someone simply told them this without either a demonstration or the opportunity to find out for themselves, the impact would be far weaker. On the negative side, discovery can be enormously time-consuming, can sometimes lead to incorrect conclusions, and can follow numerous false trails. Unsupervised discovery could even, in certain circumstances, be dangerous, for example if children were using power tools, exploring the environment, or engaging in quick physical movement.

Didactic teaching – direct information-giving – has the advantage of enabling the teacher to cover a great deal of ground quickly, to control the subject matter being learned, to make sure that it is correct and based on what has been learned by previous generations, and to short-cut a lot of anguish. The negative side is that children may merely be able to reproduce notions and facts that are ill understood. The process may have engendered no commitment or excitement.

The problem with polarising this kind of debate is that it presupposes that there is no alternative but to belong to one extreme or the other. Many teachers are able to set up conditions whereby children discover things that, to experienced adults, are entirely predictable. It is a guided activity, not true originality. No well-informed adult will be surprised if a pupil 'discovers' that a strong magnet can pick up a whole chain of loose paper clips. If a class discovered time travel then that would be a real, though highly unlikely, piece of originality.

A programme of teaching based entirely on unstructured discovery would be disastrous. If every generation of children had to find out for itself how to solve quadratic equations, that water consisted of two atoms of hydrogen and one of oxygen, that penicillin can cure certain infections, or how to build a suspension bridge or an aircraft, then progress would occur only very slowly, if at all. What has been learned by previous generations can be used as a basis on which present and future generations can build. Collecting, analysing, synthesising and communicating the accumulated wisdom of the world is a vital task in our civilisation. Since no one can know all there is to know, being able to find out for yourself, and discover novelties, alone or with others, is a vital skill in our society.

In this context, explaining takes on different forms: when *telling* someone, the teacher takes the lead, structures the information, sequences it, selects the examples, makes the summary; when *discovery* is stressed, pupils are expected to share in the shaping of the explanation, as some matters they will explain to themselves or each other, and certain issues they will bring to the teacher for an explanation. Here is a little 'experiment' you can try in order to see how children respond to approaches that involve discovery, or being told, or a mixture.

There are many variations you can invent for this kind of 'experiment'. It is an intuitive rather than a scientific method, giving you a chance to exercise professional judgement; however, the principal aim is to try out structured, semi-structured and unstructured or loosely structured approaches to see what works well. You might find, for example, that 'discovery' takes more time, but leads to more commitment and interest; alternatively, that 'telling' leads to the learning of correct information while 'discovery' leads to misconceptions. By trying different approaches with an open mind, you can widen your repertoire of professional skills, and also decide when and in what context it makes more sense to give information and when it is worth engaging in discovery. It would be a dreary teacher who did not do both at some time or other.

Activity 14

It is worth trying out two or three different approaches occasionally, not solely to see which is arguably more 'effective' in the context, but to see what is the outcome of contrasting styles of explanation. Try to teach each 'method' with equal enthusiasm and also with a group of comparable size and ability. Here are three suggestions:

(i) Magnetism

Method A   Tell a class of children about magnets. Do most of the talking yourself.

Method B   Select a dozen different objects (as described on page 23). Explain to a group of children that they should put the objects into 'Yes' and 'No' piles, depending on whether or not they think a magnet will pick up each object (paper clip, plastic rod, perspex, copper, etc.). Then they should use their magnet to test out their theory and rearrange the piles if necessary.

Method C: Give each child a magnet. Ask them to discover what magnets do and do not pick up by any method they choose (i.e. you do *not* provide any objects or suggestions yourself). See what the outcome is and what conclusions they reach.

(ii) Shapes

Method A   Tell the group they must draw a diagram which contains a circle, a triangle, a rectangle and a line. You will describe it to them (but do not show them the diagram), then tell them what to do, for example, 'Draw a tall rectangle about two inches across and four inches high … now draw a small circle touching the left-hand and bottom lines … draw a one-inch triangle on top of … ', etc.

Method B   Begin as above, but tell the group that they must ask you questions about each of the four shapes – where they are, how big, what relationship they have to one another. So someone might ask, 'Where is the triangle?' or 'How big is the circle?'

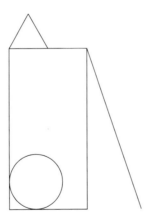

(iii) Island of Zarg

Method A   Take the map of the Island of Zarg shown on page 31. Give each child a copy and then tell them about the main features on the island. Ask them to write a story called, 'My Adventure on the Island of Zarg'.

Method B   Give them the map of the Island of Zarg, but say nothing about it. Instead tell them they must, with a partner, spend 10 minutes looking at the map and discussing what it must be like on the island, and that then they should write a story entitled, 'My Adventure on the Island of Zarg'. Make it clear that they must *not* start writing their story immediately, but rather must first 'explore' the island with the other pupil.

Evaluate each of the approaches you have used, asking questions such as:

- How long was needed for each 'method'?
- Were some approaches more time-consuming than others?
- How clear, for each 'method', were children about what they had learned?
- How involved did children appear to be under each approach?
- What did children actually learn?
- What did they remember of each activity when you asked them about it one week later?

EFFECTING CREATIVITY?

Finally, in this unit, perhaps you might like to try a much more open-ended type of explanation, where it is by no means easy to determine effectiveness. In the case of many factual or conceptual types of explanation, it is fairly simple to ask, 'Did the child learn and understand the concept?' But not all explanations lend themselves to such a straightforward assessment of their effectiveness. In the arts, in creative writing, in certain aspects of humanities topics and in personal, social and moral education, what has been learned is not easy to measure. Activity 15 gives you the opportunity to try something open ended and unpredictable and then try to evaluate it. If it does not fit in with your teaching programme it is still worth doing, as imagination should be a part of all subject work. Alternatively, it is a good activity during a tutor group session.

Helping children to become more 'creative' can seem a diffuse objective. What do we mean by 'creative'? How do we assess 'creativity'? What standards of judgement apply to a notion as vague-sounding as 'having creative ideas'? There are several possibilities you can try which involve skills of explaining that can go well beyond the routine and which challenge both teachers' and children's imagination. In Activity 15 it is important to encourage children to produce ideas, making sure that the nervous, who are often afraid to express their more unusual thoughts (in case people should laugh *at* them rather than *with* them), are given support and confidence. It is often the out-of-the-ordinary ideas that are the winners.

Activity 15

1   Try one or more of the following 'creativity' exercises.

(a)   *Inventing new buttons*

Tell the class that they are going to design hundreds of buttons. Draw a 10 x 10 chessboard shape on the board, leaving space for more than ten ideas on either side. Explain that children must suggest *shapes* for buttons (round, square, star-shaped, tree-shaped, etc.) and these will be written along the top. Next ask for *materials* for buttons: plastic, wood, metal, carrot (they have just invented the first edible button) or whatever children suggest. Each square of the chessboard shape thus contains a button idea, from the conventional 'round, plastic' to the more unusual 'flower-shaped, metal', to the way-out 'Great Britain-shaped, chocolate', depending on what has emerged. Look through all the ideas – some will be familiar (round, plastic) but some will be novel. Do not reject the offbeat ones out of hand.

(b) *Inventing new ice-creams*

As in the buttons exercise, but substitute 'flavours' and 'add-ons' as the two dimensions, e.g. chocolate with nuts, vanilla with raisins, tomato with onion, etc.

(c) *Improving a toy*

Take a cuddly toy rabbit, doll or teddy bear and ask the class to suggest ways to make it more fun to play with (make its ears/legs move, eyes light up, legs detachable, etc.).

(d) *What if?*

Ask the class to discuss what would happen if the world were different in some way, for example, if we had two heads; if it rained so much the streets were always a foot deep in water; if it were always freezing; if we were one inch (or twenty feet) tall; if we had eyes at the end of each of our fingers.

2   Examine the way you 'explained' in these sessions. What was your response to unusual ideas? Could you handle them? Were you threatened by them? Did they make you laugh? Did you favour certain kinds of suggestion and feel less well disposed towards others? If so, which and why?

3   Look at the ideas the pupils produced. Did they appear to be safe, orthodox, wild, or inventive? To what extent did your own contribution shape the nature of the ideas being produced?

4   How can what you have learned from this exercise influence your explaining in a more orthodox context?

Unit 6 Feedback

Most people find it frustrating, if they have done something, when they don't get any feedback about it: you cook a meal and no one thanks you for it, or says it tasted nice; you perform in a play or concert and the audience remains silent at the end; you write a report and it is simply put in a drawer without comment. One of the most important elements in skilful teaching generally, not solely in explaining, is being able to act on signals and messages about how effectively or ineffectively pupils are learning. Knowledge of results, or 'feedback' as it is commonly termed, can and should influence each stage of an explanation. For example, suppose you have to explain to children about a field trip to see some interesting geographical and ecological features at a seaside location. The complete explanation might include:

geographical features   rock formations, fossils, cliffs, erosion;

ecology   marine life, shellfish, seaweed, fish, birds;

commercial aspects   fishing, tourism, harbour, coastland farming;

safety matters   dangers of cliff falls, drowning, being cut off by tide;

logistics and procedures of travel   meeting points, food, times of departure and return, money needed, clothing;

educational processes   purpose of visit, preparation in class, follow-up afterwards, assignments for pupils, books, paper or pens needed, photography, video- or tape-recording.

This would involve a large number of key pieces of information. If delivered as a sustained lecture, packed with detail, much would be forgotten. Feedback becomes, therefore, an important part of the explanation, which, in this particular case, might have to take place in bite-sized chunks, with checks to see that the main points have been absorbed. Thus the teacher might ask, 'Why do you think it's worth going to look at Exmouth?' or 'What sort of interesting things do you think we'll see when we visit the coast?' This would reveal what the class already knew. It would also be wise, indeed essential, to have a prepared page or two of written information with date, cost, times, clothing and food details on it, so that parents would know what is happening. The teacher might, having discussed the arrangements, say to the class, 'Right, turn your papers over and let's see what you can remember. Susan, what time are we leaving?'

Safety aspects might need special consideration, since absolutely everybody must be crystal clear about these, so it would be especially important to check out that every individual knew what was needed. (It would be vital to gain attention for this particular matter, otherwise excited children might easily become oblivious to what might seem, from their vantage point, a less interesting aspect of the trip.) One teacher has a series of adept ways of gaining attention from excited children on field trips, including, when someone has left a watch, camera or pen lying around, saying something like, 'Who's going to claim this watch before I stamp on it?'

The teacher might ask the pupils, 'What safety rules do we need so that no one has an accident or gets lost?' Such matters as cliffs, tides, drowning and road crossing will then emerge, but if they do not, the teacher can put them forward. There might, in the end, be 'Three Golden Rules' for safety, or whatever is appropriate, and the teacher could check that each is understood and remembered. There are numerous ways of obtaining feedback, and the above represents just one set of possibilities out of millions.

EVALUATING EXPLANATIONS

Feedback can help with the evaluation of an explanation. It can take the form not only of reactions from pupils or observers to your own teaching, but also knowledge of the results of explanations given by others. This can include research findings, which, although often in generalised form, can sometimes be relevant to individuals. Principally, however, teachers improve their classroom skills by scrutinising their own strategies and, in the light of feedback, trying out other approaches that might be even more effective. Forms of feedback can include:

Personal feedback

- answers to oral questions;
- written tests of knowledge and understanding;
- children's responses to practical tasks;
- comments and insights of an observer or appraiser;
- listening to a tape or watching a video of your own lesson.

General feedback

- observing and analysing other teachers' or students' explanations;
- watching videos, reading transcripts of other teachers' lessons;

- looking at research findings;
- considering the views of those who have successful experience and expertise, or who are competent to make judgements about effective explaining.

We have already covered a number of these points in the previous five units and the various activities described in them, but soliciting and acting on feedback is such a central matter that it is worthy of as much attention as can sensibly be paid to it. The following section offers examples of possibilities for feedback under each heading.

Answers to oral questions

Sometimes pupils' answers to oral questions can reveal what it is they do not understand. A boy was asked in German during a modern language lesson 'What has twelve months?' The answer should have been 'A year', but he replied, in German, 'December'. This revealed that he did not understand, in the foreign language, the difference between 'twelve' and 'twelfth', so it needed explaining to him.

Consider the following incorrect answers to a mental arithmetic question. Pupils were asked to divide 927 by 3. Most pupils correctly answered 309, but three pupils replied 39, 308 and 30 respectively. Further investigation showed the following explanations for the errors:

1   39: A simple place value mistake. The pupil had worked out that 9 divided by 3 was 3, and then that 27 divided by 3 was 9.
2   308: An arithmetical error. The boy had done the calculation correctly until the last part and had then wrongly decided that 27 divided by 3 was 8.
3   30: A more complicated error, indeed a series of them, each compounding the other. The girl had decided to use estimation, but had also made a place value error as well. Thinking that 927 was roughly 930, she wrongly surmised that the answer must be 31. She then subtracted the 1 from her answer to compensate for the 3 she had added in the first place.

In each case, the errors and their explanations offer valuable feedback. The first pupil needs work on place value. The second has an insecure grasp of 'multiplication facts' as 'tables' are now called. The third needs to understand better what estimation involves and that it still needs to be as accurate as possible. She is also confused about place value.

Written tests of knowledge and understanding

Once in a while it is worth making the effort to devote more time than usual to *one particular* written assignment, to see what feedback can be obtained on how effective the explanatory or setting-up phase of the lesson was. For example, if

Which of these animals are insects?

Put a tick (✓) in the box beside the pictures of insects and a cross (×) in the box beside the pictures of other sorts of animal.

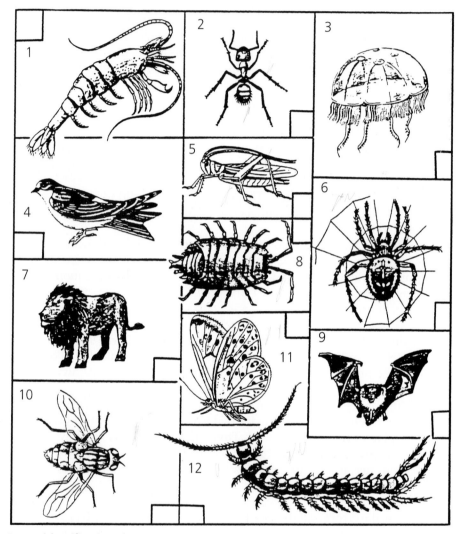

Insect identification sheet

the class has written a piece of imaginative writing, like the 'My Adventure on the Island of Zarg' exercise on pages 31–2, then a more elaborate than usual marking and grading scheme might be used, looking at such features as: length of story; structure of sentences and whole piece; vocabulary; coherence and organisation of story (whether it was easy or hard to follow the storyline); which features of the island were mentioned; imaginativeness; grammatical and syntactical accuracy and punctuation and spelling. It is not easy to relate each of these to the teacher's initial explanatory introduction, but it is worth taking note whether children merely reproduced ideas that were mentioned in the interactive or narrative phase of the lesson, or were stimulated to produce their own ideas.

With more factual explanations, a different approach to written testing may be necessary. Suppose you have been explaining a new concept to a class. There are several ways in which you can obtain written feedback. If the lesson has been video-taped, or the sound recorded on a cassette recorder, then the tape can be replayed and analysed in the light of the pupils' written responses to discover why certain misconceptions or omissions might have occurred. One teacher using the approach thought she had used the term 'thorax' when describing the middle section of insects' bodies, but discovered (a) that only one pupil knew the word in the test, (b) on playback of the video she realised that she had never mentioned the term.

An identification sheet   Compile a sheet of ten or twelve pictures of objects that illustrate the concept being studied. For example, if the class had been studying insects, then the sheet could contain pictures of creatures like a butterfly, a house-fly and a cricket (which are insects) and a woodlouse, a spider and a bat (which are not). Ask children to put a tick or cross by each one. A study of the errors, and of a tape, if available, would reveal what misconceptions have occurred.

Sentence completion   Draw up a set of sentences with gaps like:

'An insect has (no, two, four, six, eight) legs.'

'Its feelers are on its (body wings, tail, head).'

'The thorax is in the (middle, front, tail) of an insect.'

Diagram   Ask the children to draw and label a picture of an insect, putting in the following terms: head, wings, legs, feelers, thorax, abdomen.

Narrative explanation   Give the instructions: 'Peter comes from a country where there are no insects at all. Write a few sentences telling him what insects are.'

Activity 16

1   Set up some kind of practical task. It could be a scientific experiment, a role-play in a modern languages lesson, a technology assignment or composing and performing a piece of music. Video or sound record the setting up and initial explaining phase of the lesson.

2   After the lesson, look at the end results. Do the pupils appear to have grasped and applied the principles and processes you explained? Did any individual or group have major or minor misconceptions about the nature and purpose of the activity?

3   Study the video- or audio-tape. Are there any clues about why any confusion, errors or misconceptions may have occurred? If the activity went well, are there identifiable reasons why your explanation phase may have been particularly clear, like an effective demonstration, a successful engagement of interest and curiosity, a whetting of appetite, a clear focus on the sequence of events to be followed?

Analysing your own or other people's explanations

We have already discussed the analysis of explanations in Unit 3. However, either when an observer is watching you or if you are studying a tape, transcript or video in your own lesson, you can focus on one or more specific aspects and obtain feedback which will help you to improve your skill.

Take, for example, the notion of opportunity to learn, that is, children having the chance during a lesson to learn some particular feature. The teacher mentioned above thought she had used the term 'thorax' in her exposition, but analysis of the tape showed she had forgotten to introduce this new word. In other words, the class had been denied the opportunity to learn it. The boy who did know it had met it in a book. The book had been his opportunity to learn.

We have often found the same outcome in our research projects, after analysing tapes and videos of lessons and then comparing these with children's responses to test papers. Lists of key concepts were compiled and observers checked each lesson video to see if children had had the opportunity to read about, look at, discuss, be told or ask questions about each of these. In many cases where errors or omissions occurred, there had been no detectable opportunity to learn in the lesson.

GENERAL FEEDBACK – RESEARCH FINDINGS, EXPERT VIEWS, PUPIL VIEWS

The findings from research studies can offer, in particular, three useful forms of feedback to the individual teacher. First of all there may be certain general trends that are worth knowing about, though research into teaching and learning does not normally produce the high correlations and huge effect sizes which are found in sciences, where the experimenter can exercise tighter control over experimental conditions, such as temperature, volume or pressure, or where inert unchanging substances, rather than human beings, are involved.

However, teaching in individual classrooms can often be improved by small incremental gains, rather than by some single miracle cure-all. Professor Nate Gage, in his book, Hard Gains in the Soft Sciences (1985), tells how relatively trivial experimental effects in medicine can lead to major policy shifts. In 1982 a study was conducted on the effects of a drug called propranolol on patients who had suffered a heart attack. After thirty months, 9.5 per cent of the men who had received a placebo, or dummy pill treatment, had died, whereas only 7 per cent of those given propranolol had died.

This difference of 2.5 per cent between the experimental and control groups was regarded as so significant that the experiment was terminated and a general recommendation was made that the new drug should be available to all. The story was on the front pages of many leading American newspapers. Yet, in research on explaining in the classroom, if method A were shown to be only 2.5 per cent superior to method B, no one would dream of suggesting general application. Even slightly significant findings in research on teaching may, therefore, be at least worth considering. Lots of little effects will eventually add up to a much bigger effect.

Second, teachers can try to replicate in their own classrooms, albeit on a modest scale, a study performed elsewhere with several teachers. Activity 17 gives an example of this. Third, even if one is not convinced by findings which may be based on research in different kinds of classroom from one's own, or on research from another country, or with older or younger pupils, or on procedures with which one disagrees, there is often an idea or two which can be taken and adapted to suit one's own conditions.

For instance, irrespective of anyone else's findings about the use, during explanations, of rules and examples, individual teachers can explore their own preferences. They might try a pattern of 'rule–example–rule', then one of 'example–rule–example' or even 'example–example–rule' ('9 times 10 is 90; 23 times 10 is 230; all whole numbers multiplied by 10 end in a zero'). There is often considerable pressure for teachers to follow some favoured orthodoxy in different periods of our history, but there are always ways of modifying what someone else has done to suit individual tastes. Research findings and universal prescriptions do not solve all our questions, and they should neither be adulated uncritically, nor dismissed out of hand. Many skilful teachers are, in their daily professional work, lifelong researchers into the art and science of their own teaching.

Activity 17

Applying research in your own classroom

In order for explanations, whether by teacher or pupil, to be absorbed fully, pupils may need a little more time than they are sometimes given. Mary Budd Rowe (1978) investigated the amount of time that teachers allow children to answer a question, known as wait time. She analysed 800 tape recordings of lessons and found that teachers often asked between three and five questions per minute, but tended to allow only a second or less for a child to respond before asking someone else, or answering the question themselves, or rephrasing it.

'Wait time' (according to Mary Budd Rowe)

Teacher's question or statement		Pupil's response		Teacher's response
	1st wait time		2nd wait time	

She persuaded teachers to extend the wait time to three seconds or more, not only after the teacher's question, but also after the child's response, and she found the following results:

- The length of pupils' responses increased.
- The number of unsolicited, but appropriate, responses increased.
- Failure to respond at all decreased.
- Confidence appeared to increase.
- The incidence of speculative thinking increased.
- More child-to-child interaction occurred.
- Children made more inferences and presented more evidence for what they said.

- The number of questions asked by children increased.
- Contributions by slower-learning pupils increased.
- Disciplinary problems decreased.

Try increasing the wait time in your own lesson during interactive explanations. Do you get similar results? Or does it create more problems? Not every one of Mary Budd Rowe's results is necessarily beneficial, though many would agree that most seem to have potentially positive effects. By replicating this experiment in your own classroom, see if you learn anything worthwhile. It is advisable to explain to the children that you want to give them more time to answer, so that they see the purpose of what you are doing and feel party to it.

In our own research we have found many effects while studying explaining, a number of which have been described in the course of this book. Brown and Armstrong (1989) found that the most effective (as measured by test scores, pupil and observer ratings) explainers had more keys and more types of keys. They also made more demands on pupils' higher-level thinking. Other researchers have identified 'clarity and fluency', 'emphasis and interest', 'use of examples', 'organisation and feedback', as elements of explaining which appear to be related to pupil learning.

We have also found that when teachers were explaining factual scientific topics, they were more likely to use closed questions, explain links, give or elicit examples, use summaries and visual aids, than when they were explaining more discursive matters (Wragg, 1993). In the latter case, they were more likely to use verbal cues and engage the imagination of pupils. In an experiment where one group of 128 pupils had both factual and discursive topics explained to them, while a parallel control group of 128 did not have any preliminary explanation, the group that had had an expository phase out-performed the control group, both on factual matters and in the quality of creative writing, particularly on length, coherence and imaginativeness. 'Explaining' skilfully did seem to make a difference.

Some of the factors mentioned above apply not only to research findings, but also to the views of those with successful experience. It is always problematic deciding who is or is not arguably 'successful' at explaining. What works for one expert explainer will not necessarily work for another, but nonetheless advice from experienced practitioners is well worth seeking. It can always be discarded if it does not work. Soliciting advice, especially on specific matters, is a habit worth cultivating. Only the vain and deluded are beyond advice.

Some successful practitioners, while brilliant at doing the job, are tongue-tied when asked to explain their own success, looking dumbstruck at the very thought of dissecting the intuitive and self-evident, as they see it. In such cases it is more fruitful to ask them specific questions, such as, 'How would you explain when to add and when to multiply probabilities to 13-year-olds?' or 'What can you do to explain the difference between "weather" and "climate"?' or 'How can you best explain the Elizabethan poor laws to modern pupils?' Good practitioners often enjoy explaining their art to others, even if they are modest about it. They probably realise that through explaining, as we said right at the beginning of this book, by 'giving understanding to others', we can all develop our own understanding and, ultimately, our own professional skills.

References

Adey, P. and Shayer, M. (1994) *Really Raising Standards: Cognitive Intervention and Academic Achievement*, London: Routledge.

Ausubel, D.P., Novak, J.D. and Hanesian, H. (1978) *Educational Psychology: A Cognitive View*, New York: Holt, Rinehart & Winston.

Bloom, B.S. (ed.) (1956) *Taxonomy of Educational Objectives: Cognitive Domain*, New York: David McKay.

Brown, G.A. and Armstrong, S. (1989) 'Explaining and explanations' in Wragg, E.C. (ed.) *Classroom Teaching Skills*, London: Routledge.

Bruner, J.S. (1966) *Toward a Theory of Instruction*, Cambridge, Mass.: Harvard University Press.

Cruickshank, D.R. and Metcalf, K.K. (1994) 'Explanation in Teaching and Learning' in Husen, T. and Postlethwaite, T.N. (eds) *International Encyclopaedia of Educational Research* (second edition), 10: 6143–6148, Oxford: Pergamon.

Gage, N.L. (1968) *Explorations of the Teacher's Effectiveness in Explaining*, Stanford University.

—— (1985) *Hard Gains in the Soft Sciences*, Bloomington, Ind.: Phi Delta Kappa.

Harrison, C. (1996) *The Teaching of Reading: What Teachers Need to Know*, Shepreth: United Kingdom Reading Association.

Howe, M.J.A. (1999) *Genius Explained*, Cambridge: Cambridge University Press.

Leat, D. (1998) *Thinking through Geography*, Cambridge: Chris Kington Publishing.

Ogborn, J., Kress, G., Martins, I and McGillicuddy, K. (1996) *Explaining Science in the Classroom*, Buckingham: Open University Press.

Piaget, J. (1954) *The Construction of Reality in the Child*, New York: Basic Books.

Rowe, M.B. (1978) *Teaching Science as Continuous Enquiry*, New York: McGraw-Hill.

Taba, H. (1966) *Teaching Strategies and Cognitive Functioning in Elementary School Children*, USOE Cooperative Research Project No.1574, San Francisco: San Francisco State College.

Vygotsky, L.S. (1978) *Mind in Society: the Development of Higher Psychological Processes*, Cambridge, Mass: Harvard University Press.

Wood, D., Bruner, J.S. and Ross, G. (1976) 'The role of tutoring in problem solving', *Journal of Child Psychiatry and Psychology*, 17, 89–100.

Wragg, E.C. (ed.) (1989) *Classroom Teaching Skills*, London: Croom Helm.

—— (1993) *Primary Teaching Skills*, London: Routledge.

—— (1999) *An Introduction to Classroom Observation*, second edition, London: Routledge.

Learning to Teach Subjects in the Secondary School Series

Edited by Susan Capel, Marilyn Leask and Tony Turner

Designed for all students learning to teach in the secondary school and particularly those on school-based initial teacher training courses, the books in this series complement our best-selling textbook *Learning to Teach in the Secondary School* and its companion *Starting to Teach in the Secondary School*.

Learning to Teach in the Secondary School
A Companion to School Experience   2nd Edition
Susan Capel, Marilyn Leask and Tony Turner

1999: 504pp
Pb: 0–415–19937–9: £16.99

The series also includes:

Learning to Teach Geography in the Secondary School
A Companion to School Experience
David Lambert and David Balderstone

2000: 516pp
Pb: 0–415–15676–9: £18.99

Learning to Teach Science in the Secondary School
A Companion to School Experience
Tony Turner and Wendy DiMarco

1998: 352pp
Pb: 0–415–15302–6: £16.50

Learning to Teach Design and Technology in the Secondary School
A Companion to School Experience
Gwyneth Owen-Jackson

2000: 184pp
Pb: 0–415–21693–1: £16.99

Learning to Teach RE in the Secondary School
A Companion to School Experience
Edited by Andrew Wright and Anne-Marie Brandom

2000: 336pp
Pb: 0–415–19436–9: £16.50

Learning to Teach Art and Design in the Secondary School
A Companion to School Experience
Edited by Nicholas Addison and Lesley Burgess

2000: 392pp
Pb: 0–415–16881–3: £16.99

Learning to Teach English in the Secondary School
A Companion to School Experience
Jon Davison and Jane Dowson

1997: 352pp
Pb: 0–415–15677–7: £16.50

Learning to Teach History in the Secondary School
A Companion to School Experience
Terry Hadyn, James Arthur and Martin Hunt

1997: 320pp
Pb: 0–415–15453–7: £16.50

Learning to Teach Mathematics in the Secondary School
A Companion to School Experience
Edited by Sue Johnston-Wilde, Peter Johnston-Wilde, David Pimm and John Westwell

1999: 288pp
Pb: 0–415–16280–7: £16.50

**Learning to Teach ICT in the
Secondary School**
A Companion to School Experience
Edited by Marilyn Leask and Norbert Pachler

1999: 296pp
Pb: 0–415–19432–6: £16.50

**Learning to Teach Modern Foreign
Languages in the Secondary School**
A Companion to School Experience
Norbert Pachler and Kit Field

1997: 416pp
Pb: 0–415–16281–5: £16.50

**Learning to Teach Physical Education
in the Secondary School**
A Companion to School Experience
Susan Capel

1997: 368pp
Pb: 0–415–15301–8: £16.50

**Starting to Teach in the
Secondary School**
A Companion for the Newly Qualified
Teacher
Susan Capel, Marilyn Leask and Tony Turner

1996: 320pp
Pb: 0–415–13278–9: £16.50

*All these books are available from your normal bookshop or supplier. If you
require further information, or the RoutledgeFalmer catalogue, please call
Huw Neill on +44 0207 842 2152, or look at our website on
www.routledgefalmer.com*

Photocopiable Practical Resources for Secondary Schools

NEW

Stress Management Programme for Secondary School Students

Sarah McNamara

This is a resource pack for teachers to use in classrooms to help students combat stress. More and more young people suffer from stress nowadays, some of it school-related, some of it generated from home or friends. There are many causes, be it revision or exam pressure, bullying, low self-esteem, family problems, relationship problems, eating disorders or something else. Teachers are often the first people to notice this stress manifest itself and are more than likely the people who will have to deal with it.

As well as theory, this book has photocopiable worksheets included with it. The information is presented in an accessible way and there are plenty of follow-up activities and strategies for coping. Everything is geared towards making it readable and interesting for young people and teachers, but it never loses sight of the curriculum.

January 2001: A4: 112pp
Pb: 0–415–23839–0: £29.99

Using Data for Monitoring and Target Setting
A Practical Guide for Teachers

Ray Sumner and Ian McCallum

Are you keeping track of standards in your school?

A clear and practical guide to teachers and school administration staff that shows how to use spreadsheets and create orderly records of assessment. These can be used for the sort of statistical analyses that are now being demanded from schools. This photocopiable guide includes practical examples, step-by-step instructions, simple advice on how to use EXCEL and pictures of the actual screens you will be using.

1999: 100pp
Pb: 0–415–19686–8: £27.50

All these books are available from your normal bookshop or supplier. If you require further information, or the RoutledgeFalmer catalogue, please call Huw Neill on +44 0207 842 2152, or look at our website on www.routledgefalmer.com

Classroom Behaviour Management Titles from RoutledgeFalmer

NEW
Educating Children with AD/HD
A Teacher's Manual

Paul Cooper and Fintan O'Regan

Attention Deficit/Hyperactivity Disorder (AD/HD) is the most common behavioural disorder affecting up to 5% of children in the UK. This book provides a concise and comprehensive guide to educating children with AD/HD. It offers a theoretical introduction to AD/HD and practical guidance to the classroom teacher on how to support children with this condition.

The book is rooted in the experience of practitioners who work on a daily basis with children with AD/HD, and draws upon up-to-date research evidence on the topic. The authors challenge crude assumptions about AD/HD and argue that the best way to understand AD/HD is as a condition in which biological and environmental factors interact. Suitable for use as a teaching manual and a training resource, *Educating Children with AD/HD* will help teachers, other educational workers and students develop a sense of empowerment in relation to AD/HD to teachers.

June 2001: 112pp
Pb: 0–415 21387–8: £25.00

Surviving and Succeeding in Difficult Classrooms
Paul Blum

Focusing on the secondary school, but of great value to classroom teachers everywhere, this book offers sensible, practical advice on what to do to survive and succeed in the face of troublesome classroom behaviour.

'This is an excellent book in that it provides guidance to new teachers on the foundation of good classroom behaviour management and it is also recommended reading for staff tutors wishing to provide mentoring support for colleagues.' – *School Leadership and Management*

'This is a book for teachers ... nobody before has managed to convey the extent and degree of ill-discipline with such clarity.' – Peter Kingston of the *Guardian*

1998: 160pp
Pb: 0–415–18523–8: £12.99

All these books are available from your normal bookshop or supplier. If you require further information, or the RoutledgeFalmer catalogue, please call Huw Neill on +44 0207 842 2152, or look at our website on www.routledgefalmer.com

Inclusive Education Books
from RoutledgeFalmer

Special Educational Needs in Schools
2nd Edition

Sally Beveridge

This new edition of Sally Beveridge's renowned work provides a concise but comprehensive overview of key issues in provision for children with special needs in schools, emphasising the role of the mainstream classroom teacher. This second edition looks at the numerous changes in special educational policy and practice that have taken place in the past five years. Topics covered include:

- Concepts of SEN
- The legislative framework
- The range of special educational need and provision
- Teaching approaches and organisational strategies
- Frameworks of support

1999: 160pp
Hb: 0–415–20293–0: £42.50
Pb: 0–415–20294–9: £13.99

Photocopiable Resource
The Special Educational Needs Co-ordinator's Handbook
A Guide for Implementing the Code of Practice

Garry Hornby, Gregan Davies and Geoff Taylor

'It offers clear guidelines through the assessment procedures and supplements them with helpful proformas and illustrative material ... all in all, it should enhance the educational provision offered to pupils with special needs by helping schools to implement the Code of Practice effectively.' – *Times Educational Supplement*

'Easy to read and well-organised. The *Handbook* will be a useful resource in responding to the Code and in stimulating solutions to the challenges.' – *Educational Research*

'This publication will provide concrete support in making action for SEN pupils a reality in your school.' – *Junior Education*

1995: A4: 192pp
Pb: 0–415–11683–X: £27.50

All these books are available from your normal bookshop or supplier. If you require further information, or the RoutledgeFalmer catalogue, please call Huw Neill on +44 0207 842 2152, or look at our website on www.routledgefalmer.com